teen CUISINE
new vegetarian

Matthew Locricchio *Photography by* **James Peterson**

Amazon Children's Publishing

■ ACKNOWLEDGMENTS ■

Any cookbook that's worth enough for the pages to get dirty results from a team effort, and the author is just a part of that team. From the start, this book has had the cooperation and guidance of my devoted editor, Margery Cuyler, whose dedication to quality and impeccable detail has been its guiding force. What good is a cookbook without photography that makes you want to prepare the recipes? How lucky that I have had James Peterson Studios in Brooklyn, New York, to make that happen. Jim not only brings years of experience and technical skill with his camera to the book, but an encyclopedic culinary knowledge as well. I am very fortunate to have had the chance to work with him again. Thanks to Alice Piacenza and Nathan Meshberg for their hard work in the studio kitchen. Thanks, too, to Janet Hamlin for her drawings, to Kay Petronio for her design, and to Andrea Chesman for her copy editing.

I was also lucky to grow up in a family where good food and excellent cooks were the norm, so getting to write cookbooks has been a very satisfying way to say thank you to my mother and father. Also thanks to my family and friends who have been so supportive and patient throughout the writing of this book. In particular, I'd like to thank my niece and nephew, Virginia and Paul Zerang. Thanks, too, to sister Joanne and brothers Paul and Anthony. In addition, thanks to Guido D'Amico.

My gratitude also goes to the authors whose work inspires and informs these pages: Deborah Madison, Robin Robertson, Molly O'Neal, Andrew Schloss, Ani Phyo, Ira Chandra Moscowitz, Terry Hope Romero, and David Rosengartner, just to name a few. I also am forever grateful to the American farmers who take risks every day to provide fresh, real food to put on our tables, and whose commitment to making that happen is endless.

Text copyright © 2012 by Matthew Locricchio
Photographs copyright © 2012 by James Peterson Studio

Amazon Publishing
Attn: Amazon Children's Publishing
P.O. Box 400818
Las Vegas, NV 89149
www.amazon.com/amazonchildrenspublishing

Library of Congress Cataloging-in-Publication Data
Locricchio, Matthew.
Teen cuisine new vegetarian / by Matthew Locricchio. — 1st ed.
p. cm.
ISBN 978-0-7614-6258-3 (hardcover) — ISBN 978-0-7614-6259-0 (ebook)
1. Vegetarian cooking. 2. Teenagers—Nutrition. 3. Cookbooks. I. Title.
TX837.L63 2012
641.5'636—dc23   2011049502
Book design by Kay Petronio
Editor: Margery Cuyler

Printed in Malaysia (T)
First edition
10 9 8 7 6 5 4 3 2 1

Amazon Children's Publishing

For R.K.F.

CONTENTS

Introduction 6
Before You Begin: A Word about Safety 9

SMART STARTS
French's Toast 12
Quinoa and Whole-Wheat Bread 15
Quinoa 18
Cheddar Cheese and Jalapeño Corn Muffins 19
Crispy Tortillas and Scrambled Eggs Mex-Tex 23
Black Bean Hash Browns 25

BETWEEN THE SLICES
The New BLT Sandwich 30
Sloppy Jane. 33
The New Tempeh Burger. 37

SNAZZY SIPS
Banana Slap. 43
Strawberry Lassi. 44
Ginger Syrup 45
Ginger Ale. 47
Banana-Berry Blender Bender. 49

SUSHI-ON-A-ROLL
Sushi Rice. 52
California-on-a-Roll 55
Tempeh Fingers 59

PARTY HEARTY FOODS
Guacamole 62
Tempeh Nuggets 65
Smart Bars 69

BOWL ME OVER
The New Bean Soup 74
Homemade Vegetable Stock 77
Minestrone 79
Bite-Me Chile 85
Seasoned Croutons. 87

SALAD TOSSES

The New Waldorf Salad. 90
Red, White, and Blue Cheese Potato Salad 93
TLC Dressing 96
Rancho Dressing 97
Red Cool Slaw 99

PASTA AND POLENTA PERFECTS

Spring Table Pasta. 104
Three-Cheese Polenta Pie. 107
Instant Polenta. 110
Make-A-Scene Pasta 111
Make-A-Scene Pasta Raw Version. 115

BIG PLATES

Curried Vegetable Stir-Fry. 120
Sweet-and-Sour Tofu Stir-Fry 123
Ratatouille. 125
Eat Loaf 131
Chunky Mushroom Gravy. 134
Hodgepodge 137
Spinach Pie 141
Phyllo Dough 145

AND ON THE SIDE

Crispy Cucumber and Carrot Pickles. 149
Cucumber and Radish Relish 151
Ketchup 155
Salsa Verde 157
Carrot and Mint Chutney 161

JUST DESSERTS

Chocolate Cupcakes 167
Chocolate Cream Frosting 170
Vanilla Frosting. 171
Vanilla Cupcakes. 173
Snappy Ginger Cookies 177
Blueberry and Dried Cherry Crumble. 179

Kitchen Essentials. 182
Metric Conversion Chart 197
Kitchen Equipment and Utensils. 198
Index. 202

LIFELONG VEGETARIANS OR CURIOUS FIRST TIMERS— are you hungry for great recipes? Then this book is for you. *Teen Cuisine New Vegetarian* is all about vegetables becoming delectables. This book reinvents vegetarian cooking for all types of vegetarians and all lovers of good food. It transforms dull standards into standouts and the flavorless into fabulous. How about a bowl of Bite-Me Chile (page 85) or a Banana Slap (page 43) to get your taste buds twitching?

Even though today's teens are looking for meat alternatives, they don't want to give up indulging in delicious foods. And for good reason. A great meal prepared and shared is still one of life's enormous pleasures. So what's a veg-curious cook to do?

The most common type of vegetarian eats no meat at all. But there are also some people who consider themselves mostly vegetarian. These vegetarians, or flexitarians, eat mainly vegetable dishes but occasionally will eat fish, chicken, turkey, and even beef. Then there are vegans. Vegans choose not to eat anything that comes from an animal. This includes meat in any form and all dairy (milk, butter, cheese, eggs, and yogurt), whether from cows, sheep, goats, or buffalo. Even honey is not vegan because it is made by bees. Vegans can eat very well, however, because besides the tantalizing assortment of vegetables, there are great nondairy cheeses, buttery spreads, vegan yogurts, and nondairy cream alternatives. There are numerous vegan recipes in this book.

Some vegetarians eat raw foods and the ingredients are not heated past 180°F. Raw foods can be labor intensive to prepare, but they can be very tasty and appealing. Cooking a raw-foods diet requires significant research beforehand to make sure the diet is balanced. Do some looking before you stop cooking!

If you're thinking about becoming a vegetarian, it is important to be knowledgeable about food and nutrition. This information is readily available, and I strongly recommend you do some research. A balanced diet of fruits, vegetables, dairy, whole grains, and legumes, such as dried beans, can provide protein, carbohydrates, vitamins, calcium, omega-3, zinc, and essential nutrients to create a nourishing and satisfying way to eat.

Teen Cuisine New Vegetarian offers an assortment of recipes that are identified under each recipe title as **vegetarian (Ⓥ)**, **vegan (ⓋⒼ)**, or **raw (Ⓡ)**.

I grew up in a family of splendid vegetable cooks. We didn't eat meat on Fridays and many other days as well. My mother was the best cook in our entire family, and vegetable cooking was one of her specialties. My father was what we called in those days a "fruit and produce man." He bought wholesale fresh fruits and vegetables from the Eastern Market in Detroit, Michigan, and distributed the fresh foods on his route of small mom-and-pop markets in the outlying rural towns. Supermarkets did not exist yet. As a kid, I was lucky enough sometimes to tag along with my father in the summer. He taught me how to select ripe, delicious fruits and vegetables.

Contemporary cooks are shouting for joy that heirloom varieties of fruits and vegetables are available and that sustainable farming on a local scale is becoming more common. When we're buying local, we are buying the freshest and tastiest ingredients. The fact that those perfect butter beans grew on a farm close to your own kitchen table tells you that you're eating fresh food. Farmers' markets are great places to meet and greet your neighbors and to shake hands with some new fruits and vegetables, too.

I suggest that you plant your own garden if you are lucky enough to have the space. Talk about eating local! Growing your own is always rewarding, even if you grow only a few pots of fresh herbs on a sunny windowsill.

When people ask me why I write for young chefs, I answer that young chefs are the future of American cooking. The teen generation of new cooks can save itself and future generations from eating frozen foods, processed foods, fast foods, additives, and microwave-dependant foods.

Once you have picked your recipes, shopped for excellent ingredients, and set aside the time to cook, you're ready to have some fun. Cooking is huge fun. It can also be hard work, but the pure pleasure of cooking a successful meal is like nothing else. And every time you try a new recipe, it gets even easier.

You don't have to be a vegetarian in order to cook like one. Vegetables can stand alone as great cuisine. Discover the beauty in the unlimited assortment of vegetables that are available, and the endlessly creative ways that they can be prepared. Your own vegetarian cooking can turn out something brilliant!

Happy Teen Cuisine New Vegetarian Cooking!

A WORD ABOUT SAFETY

- Wash your hands before you begin and when you are working with food. Washing under hot water with lots of soap for twenty seconds will greatly reduce the risk of transferring bacteria from your hands to the food. Wash your hands again after you handle tofu or tempeh.

- Wash cutting boards, countertops, and equipment with hot soapy water after they've been in contact with tofu or tempeh.

- Always start with a clean kitchen before you begin any recipe and leave the kitchen clean when you're done.

- Read the entire recipe before you prepare it. You are less likely to make mistakes that way.

- Wear an apron. Tie back long hair so that it stays away from food and open flames. Why not do what a chef does and wear a clean hat to cover your hair?

- Pot holders and hot pads are essential equipment in any kitchen. The hands they save may be your own. Use pot holders, hot pads, and oven mitts only if they are dry. Using wet holders on a hot pan can cause a serious burn!

- Keep the handles of the pots and pans turned toward the middle of the stove. That way you won't accidentally hit them and knock them over. Always use pot holders to lift a hot lid or to move a pan on the stove or in the oven.

- Remember to turn off the stove and oven when you are finished cooking.

Knife Safety

- Always hold a knife handle with dry hands. If your hands are wet, the knife might slip. Think of your hands as a team. One hand grips the handle to operate the blade while the other guides the food you are cutting. The hand holding the food should never come close to the blade of the knife. Go slowly. There is no reason to chop very fast.

- Work on a cutting board, never on a tabletop or countertop.

- Never place sharp knives in a sink full of soapy water, where they could be hidden from view. Someone reaching into the water might get hurt.

- Take good care of your knives. Chef knives should be washed by hand, never in a dishwasher.

SMART STARTS

FRENCH'S
TOAST • 12

QUINOA AND
WHOLE-WHEAT
BREAD • 15

QUINOA • 18

CHEDDAR CHEESE
AND JALAPEÑO CORN
MUFFINS • 19

CRISPY TORTILLAS
AND SCRAMBLED EGGS
MEX-TEX • 23

BLACK BEAN HASH
BROWNS • 25

FRENCH'S TOAST

Ⓥ VG

There is a legend that in 1724 a tavern owner named Joseph French in Albany, New York, invented a golden, crispy breakfast dish that had nothing to do with France at all. It started when he created the recipe for what we now call French toast, and he discovered it was a hit. Modestly, he named the dish after himself. One problem, however, was that he'd never learned how to use an apostrophe. After calling his new recipe French toast (instead of French's toast), 287 years of confusion followed. Since I live in the state of New York, I thought it high time to pass on this legend and try a new version of the recipe. So here it is with its original name—but prepared 21st-century style.

SERVES 4

8 (½-inch-thick) slices Quinoa with Whole-Wheat Bread (page 15) or day-old white, whole wheat, Italian, or French bread

¼ cup raw almonds

½ cup unsweetened coconut milk

3 tablespoons safflower, canola, or peanut oil

1 tablespoon cornstarch

2 tablespoons raw (turbinado) or light brown sugar

1½ teaspoons pure vanilla extract

1 teaspoon ground cinnamon

¼ teaspoon ground nutmeg

2 cups unsweetened almond milk

Pure maple syrup, for serving

On your mark . . .

- Preheat the oven to 425°F with a rack in the middle of the oven.

- Lay the bread slices in a glass baking dish large enough to hold the slices in one layer and set aside. If you don't have a dish that size, stack the slices in pairs.

Get set . . .

- Pour the almonds into a blender. Add the coconut milk and 1 tablespoon of the oil. Press the lid firmly place. Blend on high speed for 1 minute, or until the nuts are pulverized.

- Remove the lid and add the cornstarch, sugar, vanilla, cinnamon, nutmeg, and almond milk. Press the lid firmly in place and blend for 1 minute, or until the batter is smooth and foamy.

- Pour the batter over the slices. Turn the slices to coat the other sides. Let the bread soak in the batter for 10 minutes. Every few minutes, turn the bread over to make sure all the slices are soaked with batter.

Cook!

- Coat a nonstick or heavy aluminum 10½- by 15½-baking sheet with 1 tablespoon of the oil. Place next to the stove.

- Heat the remaining 1 tablespoon of oil in a large 12- to 14-inch nonstick or heavy bottom skillet or pancake griddle over medium heat for 1 minute, until the oil is hot but not smoking.

- Lay slices of the soaked bread in the skillet or on the griddle. Don't overcrowd. It is best to cook the toast in batches.

- Cook undisturbed for 5 minutes or until browned and crispy. Turn the bread slices and cook for 2 to 3 minutes or until browned. If the toast begins to burn, lower the heat.

- Lay the browned slices on the prepared baking sheet and repeat the steps above until all the slices are browned on both sides.

- Place the baking sheet on the middle rack of the oven and bake for 10 minutes. Turn the slices and bake an additional 5 minutes.

- Serve warm with maple syrup.

QUINOA AND WHOLE-WHEAT BREAD

(V) [VG]

What's a cookbook of plant-based recipes without a really good bread recipe? This one totally fits the bill. It delivers a delicate crunchy crust with a satisfying flavor and texture, and it's healthy, too. Use this bread to make French's Toast (page 12) or for The New BLT Sandwich (page 30). The shape of the loaf makes for easy, uniform slicing. Or just bake a loaf for a smart start to your day.

MAKES 1 LOAF

1 cup warm water (100°F to 110°F), plus more as needed

1 1¼-ounce package active rapid rise yeast

1¼ cups whole-wheat flour

2 cups spelt flour or unbleached flour, plus extra for kneading

2 teaspoons salt

1 cup cooked Quinoa (recipe follows)

1 tablespoon safflower oil, plus more for the bowl and top of loaf

1 tablespoon dark molasses

On your mark . . .

- Pour ¼ cup of the warm water into a small bowl. Make sure the water is not too hot, which would stop the yeast from becoming active, or too cool, which would keep it from starting. Use a kitchen thermometer or run the water over your fingers for a few seconds to make sure it is just warm. Set aside the remaining ¾ cup water.

- Sprinkle the yeast over the water, give it a stir, and cover it. The water-and-yeast combination will need 10 minutes to become active. The yeast is active when small bubbles appear on the surface of the water. If the bubbles do not appear, you'll need to start over with a new package of yeast and fresh water.

Get set . . .

- Fit a food processor with the all-purpose blade. Add the flours and salt to the bowl. Close the lid and pulse five or six times to combine.

- Remove the lid and pour the yeast mixture into the food processor. Use a rubber spatula or spoon to make sure you get all of it. Close the lid and pulse seven or eight times to combine. Remove the lid, add the cooked quinoa, and pulse another seven or eight times.

- Combine the remaining ¾ cup warm water, oil, and molasses in a small bowl and stir well.

- Turn the processor on and slowly pour the molasses mixture through the tall feed tube. Turn the processor off just as the dough comes together in a ball. If needed, add up to 2 tablespoons additional water to bring the dough into a ball.

- Sprinkle a tablespoon of flour on a clean work surface. Sprinkle extra flour on your hands to keep the dough from sticking to them.

- Pull the dough from the bowl and place it on the work surface.

- Begin kneading by pressing the dough away from you with the palms of your hands and folding it in half. Pick it up and give it a turn to the right or left. Work the dough over and over for 2 to 3 minutes or until smooth and springy, repeating the same action. Be sure to keep turning the dough in the same direction. Add flour as needed to keep the dough from being too sticky.

- Drizzle a small amount of safflower oil into a clean bowl and add the dough. Give the dough a few spins and turn it over to lightly coat it with the oil.

- Cover with a sheet of plastic wrap and a couple of heavy, clean kitchen towels.

- Place the dough in a warm, draft-free spot where it can rise undisturbed for 1½ hours, or until it doubles in size.

- Sprinkle a little flour on a clean work surface. Pull the dough from the bowl onto the work surface and knead for 3 to 4 minutes or until smooth and springy.

- Lightly oil an 8½- by 4½-inch bread pan. Shape the dough to fit and place in the prepared pan. Brush the top with a little safflower oil.

- Cover with a sheet of plastic wrap and a couple of heavy, clean kitchen towels.

- Place the dough in a warm, draft-free spot, where it can rise undisturbed for 1 hour, or until it doubles in size.

Cook!

- [ ] Preheat the oven to 375°F with the rack in the middle of the oven.

- [ ] Carefully remove the plastic wrap.

- [ ] Bake on the middle rack of the oven for 50 minutes, or until the top is lightly browned and the bread sounds hollow when you tap it.

- [ ] Allow the bread to completely cool on a wire cooling rack before removing it from the pan and slicing.

QUINOA
Ⓥ ⱽᴳ

MAKES 2 CUPS COOKED QUINOA

1 cup rinsed quinoa

2 cups water

On your mark, get set . . .

- Place the quinoa in a fine-mesh hand strainer and rinse well under cold water.

Cook!

- Combine the quinoa and water in a 1½-quart saucepan and bring to a boil.

- Reduce the heat to a simmer, cover, and cook until all the water is absorbed, about 15 minutes.

- Let the quinoa cool for 5 minutes, undisturbed. Remove the lid and fluff with a fork.

- Serve hot or allow to cool to room temperature.

- Cover and refrigerate until you are ready to use.

Raw quinoa ready to be rinsed.

CHEDDAR CHEESE AND JALAPEÑO CORN MUFFINS

(V)

Here is an American classic muffin with a jalapeño kick and a filling of cheddar cheese and quinoa. These muffins are really savory quick breads that make a great breakfast on their own, or they can be served with Crispy Tortillas and Scrambled Eggs Mex-Tex (page 23). Show off these muffins with some jam and butter.

MAKES 12 MUFFINS

1 tablespoon butter for muffin tin

4 ounces extra-sharp cheddar cheese

1 large egg, slightly beaten

1 cup buttermilk

1 cup stone-ground white cornmeal

1 cup spelt or unbleached all-purpose flour

1 teaspoon baking powder

½ teaspoon salt

½ teaspoon smoked or regular paprika

1 teaspoon raw (turbinado) or light brown sugar

½ teaspoon baking soda

½ cup cooked Quinoa (page 18)

1 to 2 small jalapeño chiles

1 small white onion

3 tablespoons safflower oil

On your mark . . .

- [ ] With a piece of wax paper, butter a 12-cup muffin tin and set aside.

- [ ] Using the largest holes of a four-sided grater, grate the cheese into a medium bowl. You can also grate the cheese in a food processor. Follow the manufacturer's instructions for grating. You should have 1 cup.

- [ ] Combine the egg and buttermilk in a small bowl and beat lightly.

- [ ] Combine the cornmeal, flour, baking powder, salt, paprika, sugar, and baking soda in a large bowl. Mix together with a whisk.

- [ ] Fold in the cooked quinoa, grated cheddar, and buttermilk mixture. Mix until the ingredients just come together. Don't overmix. Cover and set aside.

Get set . . .

- Preheat the oven to 425°F with a rack in the middle of the oven.

- Slip on a pair of latex kitchen gloves. Remove the stems from the chiles and cut the chiles in half lengthwise. Rinse under cold water. Scrape out the seeds with the tip of a spoon and discard. Finely chop or mince the chiles, place in a small bowl, and set aside. Rinse, dry, and remove the gloves.

- Peel and finely chop the onion and add to the chiles.

Cook!

- Place the muffin pan on the middle rack of the oven to heat.

- Heat the oil in a 6-inch frying pan over medium heat until hot but not smoking.

- Add the jalapeños and onion and sauté for 3 minutes, or until tender.

- Add the onion-and-jalapeño combination to the muffin batter along with any oil in the pan.

- Using a rubber spatula, lightly fold the ingredients together. Don't overmix.

- Open the oven and using a large hot pad, transfer the muffin pan to the stovetop or a heatproof surface. With a large spoon, ladle the batter into the hot muffin cups, filling each about three-quarters full. When you reach the bottom of the bowl, don't remix the batter.

- Return the muffin pan to the middle rack of the oven and bake for 15 to 18 minutes, until the muffins are lightly brown on top.

- Insert a toothpick or wooden skewer into the middle of one of the muffins. If it comes out clean, the muffins are done.

- Let the muffins cool in the pan for 5 minutes, or until they have pulled away from the sides.

- Tip the pan over and the muffins should fall out. Place them on a wire cooling rack to finish cooling.

CRISPY TORTILLAS AND SCRAMBLED EGGS MEX-TEX

Ⓥ

Ever wanted to go to Texas and taste Tex-Mex-style scrambled eggs? Here's a recipe that's easy and satisfying and a big first step toward the Lone-Star way of cooking. The Spanish name for it is *migas*, which means "crumbs." It is a simple dish with lots of variations, but this version is as great as Texas itself. *Yee-ha!*

SERVES 4

2 (8-inch) whole-grain, wheat, or corn tortillas

1 tablespoon safflower or canola oil

2 ripe plum tomatoes

3 scallions

1 jalapeño or serrano chile

3 to 4 sprigs cilantro

2 tablespoons butter

4 large eggs

1 tablespoon water

½ cup Salsa Verde (page 157) or any bottled red or green salsa

On your mark . . .

- Preheat the oven to 400°F with a rack in the middle of the oven.

- Lay the tortillas on a cutting board. With a pastry brush, coat both sides with the oil. Cut the tortillas into bite-size strips and let them air dry on a clean plate while you prepare the rest of the recipe.

Get set . . .

- Wash the tomatoes and cut out the stem circles at the top. Chop the tomatoes into medium chunks and set aside in a medium bowl.

- Wash the scallions, remove any dark or discolored leaves, and cut off the root ends.

- Finely chop the scallions, including 3 or 4 inches of the green tops, and add to the tomatoes.

- Slip on a pair of latex kitchen gloves. Remove the stems from the chiles and cut each chile in half lengthwise. Rinse under cold water. Scrape out the seeds with

- Drain the beans in a hand strainer and rinse well under cold water. This step is important. The better rinsed the beans, the less extra salt you will have in your finished dish. Let the beans drain and place in a bowl.

- Peel the potatoes. Using the largest holes on a four-sided grater, grate the potatoes into a large bowl.

Cook!

- Heat 1 tablespoon of the oil in a large cast-iron or heavy-bottomed skillet over medium-high heat for 1 minute. Add the chopped onion, cilantro, and bell pepper and sauté for 3 minutes, or until the onion is tender. Add the black beans and cook for another 2 minutes.

- Using a slotted spoon, transfer the sautéed vegetable mixture to a medium bowl and set next to the stove.

- Add the remaining 2 tablespoons of oil to the skillet and reheat for 2 minutes until hot but not smoking. Add the potatoes, salt, and pepper and spread in a single layer in the pan. Lower the heat to medium and fry undisturbed for 5 to 6 minutes or until the potatoes start to crisp. Stir the potatoes and cook for another 6 to 8 minutes or until crispy.

- Add the sautéed vegetables and mix together with the potatoes. Fry another 5 to 6 minutes, until any liquid in the pan is cooked away.

- Serve hot.

CHEF'S TIP

The potatoes can be boiled the night before and refrigerated to save time when preparing the recipe the next day.

BETWEEN THE SLICES

THE NEW BLT
SANDWICH • 30

•

SLOPPY JANE • 33

•

THE NEW TEMPEH
BURGER • 37

THE NEW BLT SANDWICH

Ⓥ 🆅🅶 Ⓡ

Cut into matchsticks, raw beets marinated in a citrus vinaigrette create a whole new version of a B (for beets), L (for lettuce), and T (for tomato) sandwich.

SERVES 2

1 orange

1 lime

2 tablespoons extra-virgin olive oil

2 teaspoons Dijon mustard

¼ teaspoon salt, plus more for the tomato

¼ teaspoon freshly ground black pepper, plus more for the tomato

1 medium red, yellow, or multicolored beet

1 ripe tomato

2 to 4 romaine, green-leaf, Boston, or iceberg lettuce leaves

4 slices Quinoa and Whole Wheat Bread (page 15) or your choice of homemade or store-bought whole wheat bread (optional)

2 tablespoons TLC Dressing (page 96), mayonnaise, or vegan mayonnaise

On your mark . . .

- Cut the orange in half and squeeze the juice through a small hand-strainer to catch any seeds. Discard the seeds and set the juice aside in a small bowl.

- Cut the lime in half, squeeze out the juice, and add to the bowl along with the olive oil, mustard, salt, and pepper. Whisk until combined and set aside.

Get set . . .

- Slip on a pair of latex kitchen gloves to prevent staining your hands. Wash and peel the beet.

- Cut off the stem end and any greens. (Wrap and refrigerate to save beet greens for another recipe.)

- Cut the beet in half and lay it cut side down on a cutting board. Cut each half into thin slices. Stack the slices on top of each other and cut them into thin matchstick strips. Add the strips to a small bowl. Remix and pour the olive oil mixture over the beet strips and toss to coat. Set aside for least 30 minutes, or up to 2 hours.

- Wash the tomato and cut out the stem circle at the top. Cut the tomato into ¼-inch slices, cover with wax paper and let stand at room temperature.

- Wash the lettuce leaves, shake off any excess moisture, and wrap in paper towels to dry. Refrigerate until you are ready to serve.

Assemble!

- Toast the bread slices.

- Spread the dressing or mayonnaise evenly over each piece of toast.

- Lay 1 or 2 lettuce leaves on two slices of the toast.

- Using a slotted spoon, lift half the beets from the vinaigrette and lay on top of the lettuce on one piece of bread. Repeat to place the remaining beets on the other piece of bread.

- Lay the tomato slices on top of the beets.

- Season with salt and pepper.

- Top each with a second slice of the toasted bread.

- Serve with plenty of napkins.

CHEF'S TIP

Red beets can stain, so be careful to quickly clean cutting boards and your hands after handling them.

To make this recipe raw, wrap the marinated beets and tomatoes in lettuce leaves and omit the dressing.

SLOPPY JANE

Ⓥ VG

Why should only Joe get to be sloppy? It's time for Jane to mess up the place. This sandwich-on-a-bun combines mushrooms and carrots with a kicky, spicy sauce that's just sloppy enough to live up to its name. Sloppy Jane is destined to find a place in the Sandwich Hall of Fame.

SERVES 4

1 pound mushrooms (baby portobello, cremini, white, or combination)

1 small onion

2 cloves garlic

3 to 5 medium carrots

½ cup toasted wheat germ

6 to 8 sprigs flat-leaf parsley

½ cup grated Parmesan cheese or vegan Parmesan cheese

¼ teaspoon cayenne pepper

2 tablespoons tamari or soy sauce

2 tablespoons liquid smoke

1½ teaspoons salt

½ teaspoon freshly ground black pepper

4 tablespoons extra-virgin olive oil

1 tablespoon cornstarch combined with 2 tablespoons water

1¼ cups Ketchup, homemade (see page 155) or store-bought

4 hamburger buns

FIXINGS

Red Cool Slaw (page 99)

Crispy Cucumber and Carrot Pickles (page 149)

Cucumber and Radish Relish (page 151)

Red lettuce leaves

On your mark . . .

■ If the mushrooms have dirt on them, carefully brush them clean with a dry paper towel. Don't wash them, or they will absorb the water and become soggy.

■ Coarsely chop the mushrooms into medium-size chunks and set aside in a small bowl.

■ Cut the onion in half. (Wrap and refrigerate one half to save for another recipe.) Peel the onion. Using the largest holes on a four-sided grater, grate the onion and set aside in a small bowl.

■ Slightly crush the garlic by laying the flat side of a chef's knife on the clove and pressing firmly to break open the skin. Remove the skin, cut off the root end, and discard. Finely chop and add to the onion.

- [ ] Wash and peel the carrots. Using the largest holes of a four-sided grater, grate the carrots, measure out about 1½ cups, and put into a large bowl along with the wheat germ.

- [ ] Wash the parsley, shake off any excess water, and dry by rolling in paper towels. Coarsely chop and add to the carrot mixture.

Get set . . .

- [ ] Add the grated cheese, cayenne pepper, tamari, liquid smoke, ½ teaspoon of the salt, the pepper, and 1 tablespoon of the olive oil to the large bowl with the carrots.

- [ ] Mix well to combine and set aside while you cook the mushrooms.

Cook!

- [ ] In a 12-inch skillet with a lid, heat the remaining 3 tablespoons olive oil over medium heat for about 30 seconds, until hot but not smoking.

- [ ] Add the onion and garlic and sauté for 1 to 2 minutes or until softened.

- [ ] Add the mushrooms and the remaining 1 teaspoon salt. Remix the cornstarch and water combination and scrape into the pan.

- [ ] Sauté the mushroom for 5 to 6 minutes, stirring frequently. The mushrooms will be dry at first, but as they cook, they will release liquid.

- [ ] Add the carrot mixture and ketchup to the mushrooms. Carefully stir together all the ingredients.

- [ ] Bring the pan to a gentle boil, cover, and reduce the heat to low. Simmer for 15 minutes, stirring occasionally to prevent sticking. In the meantime, preheat the oven to 350°F with a rack in the middle of the oven.

- [ ] Slice the buns in half and lay them, cut side up, on a baking sheet. Set the baking sheet on the middle rack of the oven and heat for 5 to 7 minutes or until lightly toasted.

- [ ] Spoon a generous scoop of Sloppy Jane on the bottom half and put the toasted bun on top.

- [ ] Serve hot and pass the slaw, pickles, relish, and lettuce on the side. Don't forget the napkins!

CHEF'S TIP

If you decide not to make your own ketchup, check the ingredients of the store-bought ones and choose a variety without high-fructose corn syrup.

THE NEW TEMPEH BURGER
(V) VG

Tempeh is made from cooked and slightly fermented soybeans pressed to form a cake. It is versatile because it picks up flavors from other ingredients, and it is packed with protein and important essential vitamins, minerals, and fiber. There are lots of ways it can be used in cooking. This recipe combines tempeh, mushrooms, and red bell peppers to make a great burger. The patties can be formed and refrigerated up to 24 hours before serving so the burgers will be easy to finish at the last minute. Make sure you serve them with all the fixings that make for the true burger experience. Tempeh is your friend in a meatless kitchen.

MAKES 4 BURGERS

1 small red or yellow bell pepper

2 ounces portobello or white mushrooms

8 ounces tempeh (any flavor)

½ cup panko bread crumbs

3 to 4 fresh basil leaves, or 1 teaspoon dried

2 stems cilantro

2 stems flat-leaf parsley

1 clove garlic

1 tablespoon Tabasco sauce

1 tablespoon Ketchup, homemade (see page 155) or store-bought

1 tablespoon tamari or soy sauce

1 tablespoon liquid smoke

½ cup toasted wheat germ

½ teaspoon salt

1 large egg, slightly beaten (optional)

2 tablespoons extra-virgin olive oil

1 tablespoon butter or vegan margarine

4 hamburger buns

FIXINGS
Red Cool Slaw (page 99)

Crispy Cucumber and Carrot Pickles (page 149)

Cucumber and Radish Relish (page 151)

Green or red lettuce leaves

Sliced tomatoes

Sliced cheese (optional)

Ketchup, homemade (see page 155) or store-bought, and mustard

On your mark . . .

■ Wash the bell pepper. Cut out the stem at the top and discard. Cut the bell pepper in half and remove and discard the seeds and white veins. Coarsely chop

one half of the pepper and measure ½ cup. (Wrap and refrigerate the remaining half for another recipe.)

- Fit the all-purpose blade in the food processor and add the chopped pepper.

- If the mushrooms have dirt on them, carefully brush them clean with a dry paper towel. Don't wash them or they will absorb the water and become soggy.

- Coarsely chop the mushrooms into medium-size chunks and add to the pepper in the bowl of the food processor.

- Crumble the tempeh into small chunks and add it along with the bread crumbs.

- Wash the basil, cilantro, and parsley; shake off any excess water and dry by rolling in paper towels. Chop the leaves together and add to the bowl of the food processor. If you are using dried basil, add it now.

- Slightly crush the garlic by laying the flat side of a chef's knife on the clove and pressing firmly to break open the skin. Remove the skin, cut off the root end, and discard. Coarsely chop the garlic and add it to the other ingredients in the food processor.

Get set . . .

- Add the Tabasco sauce, ketchup, tamari, liquid smoke, wheat germ, salt, and egg, if using, to the food processor.

- Snap the lid into place and pulse ten to twelve times, until the mixture just comes together.

- Transfer the mixture to a medium bowl. Use your clean hands to gently complete the combining of the ingredients.

- Shape into four equal-size patties and lay the patties on a plate. Brush both sides of the patties with 1 tablespoon of the olive oil.

- Lay a sheet of wax paper on top of the patties, cover with plastic wrap, and refrigerate for at least 1 hour, or overnight.

Cook!

- ▣ Preheat the oven to 325°F with a rack in the middle of the oven. Set a small baking sheet near the oven to use later.

- ▣ In a 10½-inch skillet, melt the butter and remaining 1 tablespoon olive oil over medium heat until hot but not smoking.

- ▣ Brown the patties on each side for 2 to 3 minutes. Don't crowd the burgers as they brown. If the burgers start to burn, lower the heat.

- ▣ With a spatula, lift the burgers onto the small baking sheet. Cut the buns in half and place on the baking sheet. Bake in the oven for 4 minutes.

- ▣ Slide the burgers onto the buns and serve with the fixings of your choice.

CHEF'S TIP
To make the burger vegan, omit the egg and serve the burger with vegan cheese.

SNAZZY SIPS

BANANA SLAP • 43

STRAWBERRY
LASSI • 44

GINGER SYRUP • 45

GINGER ALE • 47

BANANA-BERRY
BLENDER
BENDER • 49

BANANA SLAP

(V) [VG]

This recipe takes a little planning. You have to freeze the bananas to achieve a thick richness that will make you think of a double milk shake. The flavor is a full banana slap-in-the-face, with a hint of nuttiness.

SERVES 2

4 bananas

3 pitted dates

¼ cup dried banana chips

1 tablespoon all-natural smooth peanut butter

6 ice cubes

1 cup chilled plain whole-milk yogurt or soy yogurt

On your mark . . .

- ☐ Peel the bananas and place them in a plastic bag or wrap with wax paper. Freeze the bananas for at least 1 hour, but no more than 2 hours.

Get set . . .

- ☐ Coarsely chop the dates and set aside.

Blend!

- ☐ Combine the banana chips, dates, peanut butter, and ice cubes in a blender. Press the lid firmly into place. Blend on high speed for 15 seconds, until barely mixed.
- ☐ Cut the bananas into large chunks and add to the blender, along with the yogurt.
- ☐ Blend for 30 to 45 seconds until smooth.
- ☐ Pour into tall glasses and serve cold.

STRAWBERRY LASSI

(V) VG

Need a cool refreshing drink to serve with spicy dishes? Crave the taste of strawberry? Then a lassi is for you. It's like a milk shake made with yogurt. This tangy drink is not overly sweet, so it really shows off the flavor of the strawberries.

SERVES 2

1 cup (10 to 12) fresh or frozen
    strawberries

1½ cups plain whole-milk yogurt or soy
    yogurt

⅓ cup cold water

2 tablespoons sugar

1 teaspoon ground cardamom

5 to 6 ice cubes, plus more for serving

On your mark, get set . . .

- ◼ If you are using fresh strawberries, wash them and let then drain in a colander, tossing lightly, to remove any excess water. Cut away any dark spots or soft brown sections from the berries. Remove the stems. The tip of a teaspoon works well for this. Slice the strawberries in half and put into a blender.

- ◼ If you are using frozen strawberries, let the whole berries partially thaw in a bowl. Transfer them to a blender.

Blend!

- ◼ Add the yogurt, water, sugar, cardamom, and ice to the blender in the order given and press the lid firmly in place.

- ◼ Blend at high speed for 20 seconds, or until smooth.

- ◼ Divide between two glasses and serve immediately.

GINGER SYRUP

(V) [VG]

This easy-to-make, flavor-packed syrup is so versatile that you'll want it to be one of your kitchen essentials. Covered and refrigerated, it will keep up to a month.

MAKES ABOUT 4 CUPS

4-inch piece fresh ginger

4 cups water

1 cup firmly packed raw (turbinado) or light brown sugar

1 tablespoon dark molasses

1 tablespoon pure vanilla extract

On your mark, get set . . .

- Wash the ginger but don't peel it. Cut into ¼-inch slices and coarsely chop.

Cook!

- Combine the chopped ginger, water, sugar, and molasses in a medium saucepan and set over high heat.
- Bring the mixture to a boil, stirring to dissolve the sugar.
- Reduce the heat to low and simmer, uncovered, for 20 minutes.
- Pour the mixture through a fine-mesh strainer into a heat-proof glass bowl. Let stand for 10 minutes.
- Add the vanilla and stir to combine.
- Pour the syrup into a clean glass jar and cover with a lid.
- Refrigerate for at least 1 hour, or overnight.

CHEF'S TIP

Fresh ginger is naturally spicy. When it is concentrated in syrup, as in this recipe, it may be too strong for some tastes. Experiment with the amount of syrup that is best for you when you use it in other recipes.

GINGER ALE

Ⓥ VG

Ginger ale has been consumed in the United States longer than any other soft drink. This recipe proves why it has always been so popular. And you can make your own. Combine your homemade ginger syrup and club soda in a tall glass with ice. You'll taste why the real thing is very cool.

SERVES 1

2 to 3 tablespoons Ginger Syrup (page 45)

8 ounces club soda

Ice cubes

On your mark, get set, stir!

- ▢ Pour the syrup into an 8-ounce glass.
- ▢ Add the ice cubes and stir.
- ▢ Slowly pour in the club soda.
- ▢ Stir once and serve.

BANANA-BERRY BLENDER BENDER

Ⓥ VG Ⓡ

The color of this blender bender will make you think "party-party." This fruit combination is a perfect pick-me-up in the middle of the afternoon or, better yet, at the start of the day.

MAKES 2 SERVINGS

1 cup fresh or frozen blueberries

1 cup fresh or frozen strawberries, plus a few for garnish

12 Ice cubes

2 bananas

¼ cup chopped dates

2 tablespoons Ginger Syrup (page 45) (optional)

On your mark, get set . . .

- Place two 8- to 10-ounce glasses in the freezer.

- If you are using fresh berries, rinse the blueberries in a colander. Discard any that are discolored or shriveled. Transfer the blueberries to a blender.

- Rinse the strawberries and drain in a colander, tossing lightly to remove any excess moisture. Cut away any dark spots or soft brown sections. Remove the stem from the top of the berry. The tip of a teaspoon works well for this. Discard the tops. Add the strawberries to the blueberries in the blender.

- If you are using frozen berries, allow the blueberries and strawberries to thaw at room temperature for 10 minutes before putting into the blender (it will be easier on your blender).

Blend!

- Add the ice cubes to the fruit in the blender.

- Slice the bananas in large chunks and add to the blender along with the chopped dates and ginger syrup.

- Press the lid firmly in place and blend at high speed for 1 minute, or until smooth.

- Pour into the chilled glasses and serve immediately.

CHEF'S TIP

To make this as a raw drink, omit the ginger syrup.

SUSHI-ON-A-ROLL

SUSHI RICE • 52

CALIFORNIA-ON-
A-ROLL • 55

TEMPEH
FINGERS • 59

Making sushi takes patience and some practice, but the result is so delicious that you simply won't mind the work that goes into making it. As with a lot of Japanese dishes, cutting and preparing the ingredients takes most of the time.

Once you follow the basic procedures for creating a sushi roll, you will discover that you can substitute other ingredients. It also takes some practice to master the rolling technique. But it's not that hard if you don't skimp on the key ingredient—patience.

Resist the temptation to overfill the sushi rolls. If that happens, you won't be able to successfully close the roll, and you'll end up with something closer to a rice salad than a sushi roll.

SUSHI RICE
(V) VG

Medium or short-grain rice contains more starch than long-grain rice. That's what makes it sticky. Sushi rice combines here with a lightly sweetened rice vinegar dressing that holds the rice together and makes it easy to roll with the other ingredients.

MAKES 2 CUPS COOKED RICE

RICE
1 cup medium- or short-grain sushi rice

2½ cups water

DRESSING
½ cup rice or apple cider vinegar

1½ teaspoons salt

2 teaspoons sugar

SEASONING MIX
1 tablespoon toasted white or black sesame seeds

1 tablespoon raw sunflower seeds

On your mark, get set . . .

- Put the rice in a fine-mesh strainer and rinse with cold water for 30 to 40 seconds. Shake the strainer frequently and continue to rinse until the water runs clear.

- Drain the rice well and pour it into a 1-quart pan and add the water.

Cook!

- Bring the water to a boil over high heat.

- Reduce the heat to a simmer, cover the pan, and cook for 20 minutes. Set a timer so you don't forget.

- To make the dressing, combine the vinegar, salt, and sugar in a small bowl and set aside.

- Using a large, wide wooden spoon, gently empty the rice into a shallow wooden, stainless steel, or ceramic bowl. Immediately sprinkle the vinegar dressing over the hot rice.

- Combine the sesame and sunflower seeds and sprinkle on the rice.

- Using the wooden spoon, gently cut lines through the rice to help it cool. Be careful not to mash it down.

- Let the rice come to room temperature. To move the cooling process along, fan the rice with a stiff piece of cardboard or a fan. Don't put the rice in the refrigerator to cool or it will become gummy.

- Once the rice has cooled to room temperature, lay a clean damp cloth over the bowl to prevent the rice from drying out.

- The rice is now ready for making sushi.

CALIFORNIA-ON-A-ROLL

Ⓥ ⓋⒼ

If you have never made sushi before, this is a good recipe with which to start. You will need a sushi rolling mat to form the sushi rolls. The mats are available at Asian markets, well-stocked supermarkets, kitchen stores, or online. You might have to try this recipe a few times before you master it. Practice makes perfect when it comes to sushi.

MAKES 2 ROLLS

1 cucumber

1 medium-size carrot

1 lemon

1 ripe avocado

1 cup water

2 full-size nori sheets (seaweed)

2 cups cooked Sushi Rice (page 52), at room temperature

Wasabi paste, at room temperature

4 Tempeh Fingers (page 59), at room temperature

Pickled ginger, for serving

Soy sauce, for dipping

On your mark, get set . . .

- ☐ Peel the cucumber. Slice it in half lengthwise; scoop out the seeds with a spoon, and discard. Lay the cucumber cut side down on a cutting board. Cut the cucumber into ¼- to ½-inch-wide pieces. Cut the pieces into 4-inch long matchsticks. Lay the cucumber sticks in a bowl and set aside.

- ☐ Wash and peel the carrots. Cut the carrots in half lengthwise and lay the flat side down on the cutting board. Cut the halves into long, thin strips and then cut the strips into 3 to 4-inch pieces. Lay the cut carrots in a small bowl and set aside.

- ☐ Squeeze the juice from the lemon into a small bowl and remove and discard any seeds. Set the lemon juice aside.

- ☐ Lay the avocado on the cutting board. With the tip of a sharp knife, start at the stem end and cut lengthwise down the avocado and up the other side. Remember that there is a large pit inside, so don't try to cut through the flesh.

- Pick up the avocado, and, holding it in both hands, twist it in opposite directions to separate the halves. Scoop out the pit with a tablespoon.

- Peel away the skin and discard. Slice the avocado into ½-inch-thick slices, cut the slices in half to make them uniform in size, and lay them in a shallow bowl.

- Pour the lemon juice over the avocado slices. Cover with a sheet of wax paper or plastic wrap to keep the avocado from discoloring. Set aside.

Cook!

- Pour 1 cup of water into a small saucepan and bring to a boil over high heat. Add the carrot sticks and cook for 3 minutes.

- Remove the pan from the heat and place it in the sink. Flood the pan with cold water to stop the cooking. Drain the carrots through a sieve. Place in a bowl and cover until ready to prepare the roll.

Roll!

- Fill a bowl with 2 cups of cold water and place it on your work counter.

- Cut a piece of plastic wrap twice the size of your rolling mat and put it on your work surface. Lay the mat on top and completely wrap both sides. Smooth the plastic wrap to remove any wrinkles. Set the mat aside. The plastic wrap will keep the rice from getting trapped in the cracks between the pieces of bamboo.

- Lay one sheet of nori on the rolling mat with the smooth side facing down and the bottom edge of the nori sheet lined up with the bottom edge of the rolling mat.

- Dip your hands into the water, scoop up about ½ cup of the rice, and shape it into a ball. Lay the ball of rice on the nori sheet and, using a flat wooden spoon or your fingers, gently spread and pat the rice to cover the sheet with a layer of rice about ¼ inch thick, leaving a ½-inch margin around the rice at the bottom edge and on the sides and the top of the sheet. The nori sheet should still be partially visible through the rice. Be careful not to mash the rice down too much. You want the grains of rice to stay whole and not clump. This is a slow process so be patient.

- If the rice begins to stick to your fingers, dip your fingers in the water again.

- Using a small spoon, spread a little of the wasabi paste from right to left across the middle of the rice. Remember that wasabi paste is hot so you won't need much.

- Lay a straight line of cucumber sticks on top of the wasabi.

- Lay the avocado slices in a line next to the cucumbers.

- Lay a line of carrot sticks on top of the cucumbers.

- Place the Tempeh Fingers on top of the vegetables.

- Wet the exposed nori with a little of the water to help it seal.

- Use the bamboo mat to roll the bottom edge of the nori over the filling. As you roll, tuck in any filling at the ends of the roll.

- Pull the mat back and lay it over the roll. Now continue to roll forward as you apply pressure and use the mat to help shape and tighten the roll. Take your time so you don't tear the roll.

- Just before the roll closes up, pull out the mat and lay it on top of the roll.

- Lightly flatten the top of the roll. Run your fingers along the sides to compact the ingredients inside. Remove the rolling mat completely.

- Gently form the roll into its final shape.

- Using both hands, lift the roll and lay it seam side down on a cutting board.

- Dip the tip of a very sharp knife into the water. Tip the knife up and tap it on your work surface to get the water to roll down the blade.

- Cut the roll in the middle, making two same-size halves. Place the halves side by side. Using a gentle sawing motion, cut both rolls into three sections. Be careful not to tear the rolls.

- Arrange the pieces of sushi face up on a serving dish. Loosely cover with plastic wrap.

- Repeat the same steps to form the second roll.

- When you are ready to serve, fill small serving bowls separately with soy sauce, pickled ginger, and wasabi paste. Serve along with the sushi.

CHEF'S TIPS

Sushi rolling mats come in an assortment of sizes. Check the package of nori seaweed and get a mat that is a little larger than the sheet of seaweed. If you are unable to find a rolling mat, a double thickness of heavy-duty aluminum foil will work. You may find also that you don't need the rolling mat at all and, with some practice, can successfully roll the sushi in the nori seaweed without any rolling mat.

You can use a variety of other fresh vegetables to make your sushi. For example, zucchini spears, partially cooked green beans, red bell pepper slices, and celery spears.

Tempeh fingers

TEMPEH FINGERS

(V) [VG]

Traditionally, a lot of people use imitation crabmeat when preparing sushi. Marinated and lightly cooked flavored tempeh is a very tasty alternative for your sushi roll.

MAKES 12

8 ounces tempeh, any variety

1 lemon

1½ tablespoons liquid smoke

3 tablespoons soy sauce

¼ teaspoon salt

1 cup water

On your mark. . .

- Cut the block of tempeh into two equal halves.

Get set . . .

- Carefully squeeze the juice from the lemon and discard any seeds. Combine with the liquid smoke, soy sauce, salt, and water in a small saucepan.
- Add the tempeh.

Cook!

- Bring the liquid to a boil over medium-high heat.
- Reduce the heat to low and cook for 15 minutes.
- Turn off the heat and let the strips remain in the liquid for at least 15 minutes, or up to 1 hour.
- Remove the tempeh and reserve the cooking liquid. Cut the tempeh into slices about 3 inches wide.
- Stack the slices and cut into ¼-inch-wide strips.
- Put the tempeh in a bowl and pour in about ⅓ cup of the cooking liquid.
- Cover and refrigerate until you are ready to serve or use in another recipe.

PARTY HEARTY FOODS

GUACAMOLE • 62

TEMPEH
NUGGETS • 65

SMART BARS • 69

GUACAMOLE
Ⓥ ⓋⒼ Ⓡ

There are some party foods that invite everyone to have a good time, and guacamole is one them. The first time you try this recipe, you should follow the instructions exactly. Then once you've mastered the dish, you can adjust the ingredients to suit your taste. When you buy avocados, let them ripen fully before you use them in the recipe. An under-ripe avocado won't cut it here.

SERVES 6

½ small white onion

1 clove garlic

1 small fresh jalapeño or serrano chile, or to taste

1 medium-size ripe tomato

4 or 5 sprigs cilantro

2 limes

3 ripe avocados

1 teaspoon salt

crispy tortilla chips for serving

On your mark . . .

- ☐ Peel and finely chop the onion and garlic and combine in a medium-size bowl.

- ☐ Slip on a pair of latex kitchen gloves. Remove the stem and cut the chile in half lengthwise. Rinse under cold water. Scrape out the seeds with the tip of a teaspoon and discard. Chop into small dice and put in a medium bowl. Rinse, dry, and remove the gloves.

- ☐ Wash the tomato, cut out the stem circle at the top, and discard. Coarsely chop the tomato and add to the bowl with the chiles. Scoop up any tomato liquid that may have escaped and add to the bowl.

- ☐ Rinse the cilantro, shake off the excess water, and wrap in a paper towel to dry. Chop the cilantro and add to the bowl.

- ☐ Cut the lime in half and squeeze the juice into a small bowl. Measure out 3 tablespoons and add to the pepper-and-tomato mixture.

- ☐ Toss together the onion and garlic, chile, tomato, and lime juice.

Get set . . .

- ☐ About 30 minutes before you are ready to serve the guacamole, prepare the avocados. Lay an avocado on a cutting board. With the tip of a sharp knife, start at the stem end and cut lengthwise down the avocado and up the other side. Remember, a large pit is inside, so don't try to cut through the flesh.

- Pick up the avocado and, holding it with both hands, twist it in opposite directions to separate the halves. Scoop out the pit with a tablespoon, but don't throw it away.

- Scrape the flesh of the avocado away from the skin and add to the bowl with the tomato mixture.

- Repeat with the remaining avocados.

- Add the salt.

- Gently mash the avocados with a wooden spoon or a fork, combining all the ingredients. Don't over mash the guacamole; it should be chunky.

- Add the pits to the bowl. This will help keep the guacamole from changing color.

- Cover the guacamole with a sheet of plastic wrap laid directly onto the surface. Keep at room temperature.

Serve!

- Remove the avocado pits and place the dip in a serving bowl.

- Surround the dip with tortilla chips.

- Serve immediately.

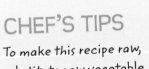

CHEF'S TIPS

To make this recipe raw, substitute raw vegetable spears for the tortilla chips.

TEMPEH NUGGETS

Ⓥ VG

These nuggets are the perfect snack to serve at the next big game or at no game at all. This recipe takes some extra steps to prepare, so plan ahead. Serve the nuggets with the dipping sauce (below) and Rancho Dressing (page 97) on the side. Get ready for a party-food touchdown!

MAKES 32 NUGGETS

NUGGETS
8 ounces tempeh, any flavor

1½ teaspoons salt

2 cups water

1 cup unsweetened almond, rice, or
 soy milk

2 tablespoons safflower or canola oil
 plus more for baking sheets

BREADING
1 cup unbleached all-purpose flour

1 cup panko bread crumbs

4 teaspoons curry powder

1 teaspoon salt

DIPPING SAUCE
¼ cup vegan margarine or butter

1 cup Ketchup, homemade (see page
 155) or store-bought

2 teaspoons liquid smoke

1½ teaspoons ground ginger

⅛ teaspoon garlic powder

1 tablespoon Tabasco sauce (add an
 extra tablespoon for super-hot
 flavor)

TO SERVE
2 stalks celery

Rancho Dressing (page 97)

On your mark . . .

- Cut the tempeh into four equal sections, cut each section in half, and then cut into 16 triangles. Put the triangles in a medium-size saucepan with 1 teaspoon of the salt and 2 cups water. Bring to a boil over medium-high heat. Reduce the heat to low and simmer, uncovered, for 15 minutes. Drain in a colander and set aside until cool.

- Slice each tempeh triangle into two halves. You will now have 32 pieces.

Get set . . .

- Combine the almond milk, oil, and the remaining ½ teaspoon of salt in a medium-size bowl. With a fork, beat for a few seconds until foamy. Add the tempeh and let stand for 10 minutes.

- Preheat the oven to 425°F with a rack in the middle of the oven.

- To make the breading, combine the flour, bread crumbs, curry powder, and salt in a large bowl and whisk together to combine.

Cook!

- To make the dipping sauce, combine the margarine, ketchup, liquid smoke, ginger, garlic powder, and Tabasco in a medium-size saucepan. Bring the mixture to a gentle boil over medium heat. Reduce the heat to low and simmer for 5 minutes. Set the sauce aside.

- Generously oil a metal baking sheet large enough to hold all the tempeh pieces in one layer.

- Lift about one-third of the tempeh pieces out of the milk and drop into the breading mixture. Gently toss with a spoon and shake the bowl back and forth to evenly coat the pieces.

- Lift the pieces onto the baking sheet.

- Repeat until all the pieces are breaded and laid on the sheet.

- Brush the oil on the top of the breaded pieces.

- Bake on the middle rack of the oven for 15 minutes.

- To serve, wash the celery stalks, trim off about ½ inch of the bottoms, and discard. Cut the stalks into 3-inch spears and set aside.

- Put the Rancho Dressing, dipping sauce, and celery sticks into separate containers on a serving tray.

- Place the tempeh pieces next to the bowls and serve hot.

Tomatillos

SMART BARS

Ⓥ

When you don't have time for breakfast or lunch, or want something different to serve at your next get-together, Smart Bars are the solution. Shop for quality dried fruits for this recipe, preferably without sulfites or other preservatives. Plan ahead so that after the bars have baked, they have time to set before you cut them. If you rush the process, the bars may crumble, making it harder to transport them. Patience will pay off. The combination of nuts, oats, wheat germ, and dried fruit come together in a classic granola bar that'll make you forget the ones that sell in supermarkets. This recipe will create a snacking legend. Now that's smart!

MAKES 16 BARS

1½ cups old-fashioned rolled oats

½ cup toasted wheat germ

½ cup raw almonds

1 cup raisins or other chopped dried fruit

½ cup dried cranberries or cherries

½ cup unsalted sunflower seeds

¼ cup chopped dates

2 large eggs, slightly beaten

¼ cup whole-wheat flour

½ cup dried blueberries or other dried berries

3 tablespoons unsalted butter

¼ cup honey or maple syrup

¼ cup firmly packed raw (turbinado) or light brown sugar

½ cup all-natural chunky peanut butter

⅓ cup unsweetened almond milk

On your mark . . .

- ▪ Generously oil the bottom and sides of a 9-inch square baking dish.

- ▪ Preheat the oven to 325°F with a rack in the middle of the oven.

Get set . . .

- ▪ Combine the oats and wheat germ in a medium bowl. Pour the mixture evenly across a dry 13- by 18-inch heavy-duty metal baking sheet.

- ▪ Bake undisturbed on the middle rack of the oven for 15 minutes. Let cool for 5 minutes, but don't turn off the oven.

- In the meantime, carefully fit the all-purpose blade in a food processor.

- Add the almonds and close the lid. Process for 15 seconds or until the almonds are finely chopped.

- Add the raisins, cranberries, sunflower seeds, and dates; process for about 15 seconds or until coarsely chopped.

- Add the eggs and flour to the food processor and process for 15 seconds.

- Transfer the fruit-and-nut mixture from the food processor to a large bowl.

- Add the oat mixture and the blueberries. Mix well to coat all the ingredients. Set the bowl aside.

Cook!

- Combine the butter, honey, sugar, and peanut butter in a small saucepan and melt over low heat, stirring until smooth.

- Add the butter mixture to the fruit mixture along with the almond milk and toss well to combine and coat all the ingredients.

- Pour the mixture into the prepared baking dish, packing it down firmly into an even thickness. A spatula will work well for this. Wet your hands and pack firmly again, pressing the mixture into the pan. The better packed the mixture, the less likely it is to crumble when you cut it.

- Bake on the middle rack of the oven for 45 minutes. It is all right if the top of the bars get browned.

- Let the bars cool on a wire cooling rack for 15 minutes.

- Cut the bars into 16 squares.

- Let them cool completely at room temperature for 1 hour, then refrigerate for at least 3 hours, or overnight.

- Wrap the bars individually in wax paper, aluminum foil, or plastic wrap and keep refrigerated until you are ready to serve. They can also be frozen.

CHEF'S TIP

You can use your favorite combination of dried fruits and seeds. Just make sure it adds up to 2 3/4 cups.

BOWL ME OVER

THE NEW
BEAN SOUP • 74

HOMEMADE
VEGETABLE
STOCK • 77

MINESTRONE • 79

BITE-ME CHILE • 85

SEASONED
CROUTONS • 87

THE NEW BEAN SOUP

(V) VG

Canned black beans are transformed into a thing of beauty when blended into this simple new version of bean soup. This recipe adds ripe avocado, fresh orange juice, and a crunchy finish of croutons for an elegant and enticing result.

SERVES 4

3 to 4 sprigs cilantro

1 ripe avocado

1 fresh orange

2 cups canned black beans

2 cups Homemade Vegetable Stock (page 77) or canned low-sodium vegetable broth

1 teaspoon salt

½ teaspoon freshly ground black pepper

1 teaspoon garlic powder (not garlic salt)

Seasoned Croutons (page 87)

On your mark . . .

- Wash the cilantro, shake off any excess water, and dry by wrapping in paper towels. Coarsely chop and set aside.

- Lay the avocado on a cutting board. With the tip of a sharp knife, start at the stem end and cut lengthwise down the avocado and up the other side. Remember that there is a large pit inside, so don't try to cut through the flesh.

- Pick up the avocado and, holding it with both hands, twist the halves in opposite directions to separate. Scoop out the pit with a tablespoon and discard.

- Peel the avocado halves and cut into slices. Put in a small bowl.

- Cut the orange in half and squeeze the juice through a small strainer to catch any seeds. You will need about ⅓ to ½ cup juice. Pour the juice over the avocado slices and use a spoon to coat the slices with the juice. Cover with plastic wrap and refrigerate until you are ready to serve. Discard the squeezed orange halves.

- Drain the beans in a hand strainer and rinse well under cold water. This step is important. The better rinsed the beans, the less extra salt you will have in your finished dish. Let the beans drain.

Get set . . .

- Place 1 cup of the beans in a blender and add 1 cup of the vegetable stock. Press the lid firmly in place. Blend at high speed until the beans have the consistency of thick cream. Some whole beans should remain.

- Pour the blended beans into a large saucepan.

- Pour the remaining cup of beans and remaining 1 cup of stock into the blender and blend at high speed for 3 to 4 seconds. Pour into the saucepan and set aside.

Cook!

- Heat over medium heat. Add the salt, pepper, and garlic powder, and bring to a boil. Reduce the heat to low and simmer for 5 to 8 minutes. Stir the soup frequently as it cooks. Using a metal spoon, skim off any foam or impurities that rise to the surface and discard.

- To serve, divide the soup among individual bowls. Top with the avocado and some of the orange juice, chopped cilantro, and croutons.

- Serve hot.

CHEF'S TIP

When shopping for canned black beans, look for those that are low in sodium.

HOMEMADE VEGETABLE STOCK

(V) [VG]

Canned vegetable stock is available, but the store-bought products are usually too sweet or too salty and may have added coloring. Sometimes the flavorings can overpower the subtle flavors of a recipe. If you make it yourself, your stock will blend into your recipe and enrich it. Who wants an unidentifiable flavor that works against the finished dish?

MAKES 2 QUARTS

6 carrots

3 stalks celery

3 scallions

6 leaves romaine, green leaf, or iceberg lettuce

8 ounces fresh white mushrooms

1 yellow onion, cut into quarters

3 slices fresh ginger, each about ½ inch thick (the size of a quarter)

10 cups cold water

On your mark . . .

- Wash the carrots, celery, scallions, and lettuce to remove any sand or dirt. Wipe off any dirt from the mushrooms with a dry paper towel. You don't have to peel the carrots or the onions—the skins will give the stock extra flavor.

Get set . . .

- Chop the vegetables into large chunks.

Cook!

- Combine the carrots, celery, onion, scallions, lettuce, mushrooms, ginger, and water in a large pot.
- Bring to a boil over high heat, reduce to low, and simmer for 1½ hours. Using a metal spoon, remove any foam or impurities that rise to the surface.
- Turn off the heat. Place a colander over a heat-proof bowl or large pot. Strain the stock through a colander. Discard the vegetables.
- Let the stock cool, uncovered, for 20 minutes. Cover and refrigerate.

CHEF'S TIP

Vegetable stock can be refrigerated in an airtight container for up to 7 days. It can also be frozen in smaller plastic containers with tight-fitting lids for up to 3 months. To thaw, place the container upside down under cold running water and press the bottom to push out the frozen stock. Place the stock in a pan on the stove. Heat, covered, over low, until the stock melts. It can also be thawed overnight in the refrigerator. To prevent the growth of bacteria, never thaw vegetable stock on the counter or at room temperature.

MINESTRONE

(V) VG

This soup is considered by many to be Italy's most famous soup. The addition of savory wild mushrooms to this vegetarian cookbook standard sets it apart from other versions. Cooking mushrooms dates back to the Greek and Roman cooks who probably used mushrooms in a large assortment of dishes. In those days, you knew you were important if you were served mushrooms. Why not show how highly you regard your guests by serving this legendary soup?

SERVES 8

1 medium-size onion

2 medium-size potatoes

4 ounces oyster, shiitake, or chanterelle mushrooms, or a mixture of each

4 small carrots, unpeeled

3 stalks celery

2 medium-size zucchini, unpeeled

¼ medium-size head Savoy or green cabbage

2 cloves garlic

1½ cups canned cannellini beans, drained

2 tablespoons butter or vegan margarine

2 tablespoons extra-virgin olive oil

1 cup canned chopped plum tomatoes with the juice

1½ teaspoons salt

½ teaspoon freshly ground black pepper

6 cups Homemade Vegetable Stock (page 77) or canned low-sodium vegetable broth

½ cup small dried pasta (seashells, mini-elbows, or ditalini)

Freshly grated Parmesan cheese, preferably Parmigiano-Reggiano, or vegan Parmesan, to serve

On your mark, get set . . .

- Peel the onion, chop into small pieces, and set aside.

- Wash the potatoes and cut in half lengthwise. Lay the flat side down and cut each half into slices. Cut the slices into small chunks and set aside.

- Using a vegetable brush or paper towel, brush off any dirt from the mushrooms. Remove the stems of the shiitake mushrooms and discard. Finely chop the mushrooms. You should have about 1 cup. Set aside.

- Using a vegetable brush, wash the carrots, celery, and zucchini. Chop into bite-size pieces and set aside.

- Remove any limp outside leaves from the cabbage. Cut out the white core at the base. Cut the cabbage into quarters and chop into small pieces. Measure 2 cups and set aside.

- Slightly crush the garlic by laying the flat side of a chef's knife on the clove and pressing firmly to break open the skin. Remove the skin, cut off the root end, and discard. Coarsely chop the garlic and add to the onion.

- Drain the beans in a hand strainer and rinse well under cold water. This step is important. The better rinsed the beans, the less extra salt you will have in your finished dish. Let the beans drain.

Cook!

- In a 6- to 8-quart pot large enough to hold all the ingredients, heat the butter and olive oil over medium-low heat.

- Add the onion and garlic. Cook for 4 to 6 minutes, stirring frequently to prevent sticking, until the onion and garlic become soft and translucent.

- Add the potatoes, mushrooms, carrots, celery, zucchini, cabbage, cannellini beans, tomatoes, salt, and pepper. Stir well.

- Cook for 10 to 12 minutes or until the vegetables are just beginning to soften. Stir occasionally. With a metal spoon, remove any foam that rises to the top.

- Add the broth. Raise the heat to medium-high and bring to a boil. Continue to skim off any foam that rises to the top as the soup cooks.

- Reduce the heat to low, cover the pot with the lid slightly ajar, and simmer gently for 30 minutes.

- Add the pasta, raise the heat to medium, and cook for another 8 to 10 minutes, until the pasta is tender.

- Serve hot and pass the Parmesan to sprinkle on top.

Oyster mushrooms

Shiitaki mushrooms

Chanterelle
mushrooms

BITE-ME CHILE

Ⓥ VG

A bowl of chile is a thing of beauty. So what's wrong with a triple dose of heat in your chile? This recipe combines three types of chiles into one big bite of zippy flavor and satisfying chile goodness. Read the chef's tip (next page) to find out how to adjust the heat level.

SERVES 4

1 pound tempeh, any flavor

1 medium-size white onion

5 to 6 sprigs flat-leaf parsley

5 to 6 sprigs cilantro

2 cloves garlic

1 to 2 jalapeño or serrano chiles

1 to 3 dried ancho, negro, or pasilla chiles, depending on taste

1 14.5-ounce can fire-roasted or regular chopped tomatoes

1 10-ounce can Ro*Tel brand diced tomatoes and green chiles

1 15.5-ounce can red pinto, great Northern, or black beans

3 tablespoons extra-virgin olive or safflower oil

1 4-ounce can chopped mild, medium, or hot green chiles

1 tablespoon chile powder

1 teaspoon smoked or regular paprika

½ teaspoon salt

½ teaspoon cayenne pepper (optional)

1 cup water, plus more as needed

CHILE FIXINGS

Chopped scallions

Chopped white or red onions

Cheddar cheese or vegan cheddar, grated

Monterey Jack or vegan Jack cheese, grated

Sour cream or vegan sour cream

Plain whole-milk yogurt or soy yogurt

On your mark . . .

- ◼ Cut the tempeh into medium-size pieces and put into a 2-quart saucepan. Cover with cold water and bring to a boil over medium heat. Reduce the heat to low and simmer for 20 minutes. Drain in a colander and set aside.

- ◼ Peel the onion, chop into medium dice, measure out 1 cup, and set aside.

- ◼ Wash the parsley and cilantro, shake off any excess water, and dry by rolling in paper towels. Remove the leaves and discard the stems. Coarsely chop the parsley and cilantro together and set aside.

- Slightly crush the garlic by laying the flat side of a chef's knife on the clove and pressing firmly to break open the skin. Remove the skin, cut off the root end, and discard. Coarsely chop the garlic and set aside.

- Slip on a pair of latex kitchen gloves. Remove the stem from the fresh chiles and cut in half lengthwise. Rinse under cold water and scrape out the seeds with the tip of a spoon. If you like the chile a bit hotter, leave in the seeds. Chop into small pieces and set aside. Rinse, dry, and remove the gloves.

Get set . . .

- Break the stem from the dried chiles and discard. Shake out any seeds, tear the chiles into small pieces, and place in a bowl. Add ½ cup hot water and set aside to soften. Wash your hands.

- Combine the tomatoes, including the liquid, and the tomato-and-green chile combination. Measure out 3 cups and set aside.

- Drain the canned beans in a hand strainer or colander. Rinse under cold water and set aside to drain.

- Coarsely chop the tempeh and set aside.

Cook!

- Drain the dried chiles in a hand strainer or colander and pat dry.

- Heat the oil in a 4- to 6-quart pot (with lid) over medium-high heat until hot but not smoking.

- Add the onion and dried chiles and sauté for 4 to 5 minutes, until the onion is soft and translucent.

- Add the garlic, tempeh, canned green chiles, chopped fresh chiles, chile powder, paprika, salt, cayenne pepper, if using, and the chopped parsley and cilantro. Cook for 5 minutes, stirring frequently to prevent sticking, until the tempeh has browned.

- Add the 3 cups tomato mixture, beans, and water. Bring to a boil, decrease the heat to low, and simmer for 45 minutes with the lid slightly ajar.

- Stir occasionally to prevent sticking. Add water if the chile becomes too thick, but avoid making it soupy. Taste the chile and correct the seasoning.

- Serve hot, passing the scallions, onions, grated cheeses, sour cream, and yogurt on the side.

SEASONED CROUTONS

Ⓥ 🆅🅶

Quick and easy to make, seasoned toasted bread cubes are the perfect crunchy topper for soups or salads.

MAKES ABOUT 1 CUP

3 tablespoons extra-virgin olive or peanut oil

½ teaspoon salt

½ teaspoon smoked paprika

¼ teaspoon freshly ground black pepper

¼ teaspoon ground oregano

6 large slices bread, such as Italian ciabatta, peasant bread, French bread, or baguette

On your mark . . .

- Preheat the oven to 300°F with a rack in the middle of the oven.

- Combine the oil, salt, paprika, pepper, and oregano in a small bowl.

- Cut the slices of bread into 1-inch-wide strips. Cut the strips into ½-inch cubes and put into a medium bowl.

Get set . . .

- Add the spiced oil to the bowl and toss well to coat the cubes.

- Lay the cubes in a single layer on a small baking sheet.

Cook!

- Bake for 20 minutes, or until golden and crispy. The baking time will depend on the size of the cubes, so be careful that they don't burn. Once or twice during baking, use a metal spoon to stir the croutons.

- Let them cool completely on the baking sheet.

- To keep the croutons crispy, store them in a clean glass jar with a lid. If stored in a plastic container, they tend to lose their crunch. The croutons will keep for up to 1 month.

SALAD TOSSES

THE NEW WALDORF
SALAD • 90

■

RED, WHITE, AND
BLUE CHEESE
POTATO SALAD • 93

■

TLC DRESSING • 96

■

RANCHO
DRESSING • 97

■

RED COOL
SLAW • 99

THE NEW WALDORF SALAD

(V) [VG] (R)

In case you've never heard of this salad, here's the story. The salad was invented in 1896 by the man who ran the day-to-day operations of the legendary and still operating Waldorf Astoria Hotel in New York. His name was Oscar Tschirky, and he was so famous in the old days that he was known simply as "Mr. Oscar." When heads of state stayed in the hotel, they would demand that Mr. Oscar wait on them. His fan base was huge and everybody clamored for his exceptional service. He created the original Waldorf Salad for the luncheons that took place before the official opening of the hotel. Mr. Oscar sure invented one keeper of a recipe! Millions of Waldorf salads have been served to happy salad lovers over the years. This old-school standard gets a whole new look and taste in this recipe, but its heart is still in the right place with Mr. Oscar.

SERVES 6 TO 8

SALAD
1 medium-size bulb fresh fennel

3 sprigs mint

1 small jalapeño chile

1 crisp apple

½ cup chopped dates

¾ cup chopped walnuts, almonds, cashews, or macadamia nuts

½ cup dried mango, papaya, apricots, cherries, cranberries, or other dried fruit

4 ounces soft goat cheese or vegan pepper Jack cheese

DRESSING
1 orange

¼ cup safflower or coconut oil

3 tablespoons rice or balsamic vinegar

½ teaspoon salt

On your mark . . .

- ☐ Cut off the top stalks and fronds of the fennel and discard. Cut out the white core at the bottom of the fennel bulb.

- ☐ Cut the bulb into thin slices and add to a medium-size bowl.

- ☐ Wash the mint and shake to remove any excess water. Pull off the leaves and discard the stems. Wrap the leaves in paper towels to remove any excess water. Coarsely chop and add to the bowl.

- ☐ Slip on a pair of latex kitchen gloves. Remove the stem and cut the jalapeño in half lengthwise. Rinse under cold water. Scrape out the seeds with the tip of a teaspoon and discard. Chop into small dice and add to the fennel-and-mint mixture. Rinse, dry, and remove the gloves.

Get set . . .

- [ ] To make the dressing, cut the orange in half and squeeze the juice through a small hand strainer to catch any seeds. Measure out ½ cup and pour into a medium-size jar with a lid.

- [ ] Add the oil, vinegar, and salt. With the lid in place, shake the dressing vigorously until mixed. Set the dressing aside.

Toss!

- [ ] Wash the apple, but don't peel it. Cut the apple in half and remove the core. Cut the apple into a combination of thin slices and small chunks and add to the fennel.

- [ ] Pour the dressing over the apple-and-fennel combination and toss to coat evenly.

- [ ] Add chopped dates and toss well.

- [ ] Add the chopped nuts and toss. Cover and set aside.

- [ ] Finely chop the dried fruits and add to the bowl. Toss well to coat all the pieces.

- [ ] Cover and refrigerate the salad for at least 15 minutes or up to 1 hour.

- [ ] Crumble the cheese into small pieces and mix into the salad.

- [ ] Serve immediately.

CHEF'S TIP

If you would like the salad extra spicy, don't remove the seeds in the jalapeño. To make the salad raw, omit the cheese. Shop for dried fruits that contain no sulfites or other preservatives.

Fresh fennel bulb

RED, WHITE, AND BLUE CHEESE POTATO SALAD

(V)

Rarely do we make a fuss about the potato's versatility, nutritional value, and smooth, satisfying taste. It is easy to digest, low in fat, has no cholesterol, and is packed with minerals and complex carbohydrates. There are less than 120 calories in a 6-ounce potato. What else can be baked, made into a cake, dried, French fried, mashed, smashed, hashed, stuffed, grilled, chilled, dilled, or served en brochette or as a croquette? A salad is a perfect way to prepare the new potatoes you just bought at the farmers' market to stand out and get noticed. Vegetable gods! Here is the potato salad to prove it.

SERVES 6

3 stalks celery hearts*

1 15.5-ounce can cannellini beans

5 to 6 sprigs flat-leaf parsley

2 scallions

3½ ounces Roquefort, Gorgonzola, Stilton, Valdeon from Spain, or other blue cheese of your choice

⅓ cup extra-virgin olive oil

1 tablespoon plus ½ teaspoon salt

1 teaspoon freshly ground black pepper

1 tablespoon rice vinegar or red wine vinegar

1 pound small, new red-skin potatoes

½ cup whole-milk yogurt

On your mark . . .

- Wash the celery stalks and leafy tops. Chop into small dice, measure 1 cup, and put into a large bowl.

- Drain the beans in a hand strainer and rinse under cold water. Shake the strainer back and forth to remove any excess water and add to the bowl of celery.

- Wash the parsley, shake to remove any excess water, and dry by rolling in paper towels. Remove the stems, coarsely chop the rest, and add to the bowl.

- Wash the scallions, cut off the root ends, and remove any dark or discolored leaves. Finely chop, including about 3 or 4 inches of the green tops. Add to the bowl.

- Crumble the blue cheese, and add to the bowl.

Get set . . .

- Add the olive oil, ½ teaspoon of salt, the pepper, and the vinegar to the salad. Toss well to coat all the ingredients. Cover the bowl with wax paper and set aside.

- Wash the potatoes by scrubbing with a vegetable brush. Cut the potatoes in half, lay face down, and cut into ¼-inch slices.

Cook!

- Put the potatoes in a large saucepan, cover with 6 cups water, and add the remaining 1 tablespoon of salt.

- Bring the pan to simmer over medium-high heat, uncovered. This will take about 12 minutes.

- Lower the heat and simmer for about 10 minutes, or until the potatoes are tender and can be easily pierced with the tip of a thin knife. Be careful the water doesn't boil too fast or the potatoes might break apart.

- Drain the potatoes in a colander. Add the potatoes to the vegetable mixture and toss gently to combine. Let the potato salad cool for about 10 minutes.

- Add the yogurt and gently toss.

- Serve immediately. If you are not serving immediately, cover and refrigerate for up to 24 hours; bring to room temperature before serving.

CHEF'S TIP

When shopping for potatoes, select ones that are firm, without blemishes, wrinkles, or cracks. Make sure they have not sprouted and avoid ones with any green skin. Don't store them in the refrigerator or the potato will darken when cooked. Keep potatoes away from bright sunlight to avoid sprouting. If stored in a cool place, they will stay fresh for up to 2 weeks. Remember, the skin of the potato has great flavor and food value, so it is okay to leave it on. Just make sure you scrub it before cooking.

* A bunch of celery consists of a dozen or so of individual stalks or ribs. The tender innermost stalks are called the celery heart. To expose it, pull away the outer ribbed stalks. Once you remove them, you will discover lighter green stalks with green leaves underneath. That is the celery heart. (Wrap and refrigerate the outer stalks and save them for another recipe.)

TLC DRESSING

(V) VG

Sometimes you need a thick, luscious, and creamy dressing to pour on slaws or salads or to serve as a dip for raw vegetables or to make as a spread for sandwiches and burgers. Here is the recipe for you, and the blender does most of the work. After you experience TLC, you'll wonder where it's been all your life.

MAKES 2 CUPS

1 cup silken tofu

¾ cup raw almonds

3 tablespoons extra-virgin olive oil

2 tablespoons untoasted white sesame seeds

¾ cup unsweetened almond milk

2 tablespoons freshly squeezed lemon juice

¼ teaspoon cayenne pepper

½ cup Ketchup, homemade (page 155) or store-bought

¼ teaspoon ground ginger

1¼ teaspoons salt

2 tablespoons balsamic vinegar

On your mark, get set . . .

- Drain the tofu in a hand strainer for 15 minutes.

- Meanwhile, combine the almonds, olive oil, and sesame seeds in a blender.

Blend!

- Press the lid firmly in place and blend on high speed for 15 seconds.

- Remove the lid and add ½ cup of the almond milk.

- Press the lid firmly in place and blend on high speed for another 30 seconds or until the mixture has thickened.

- Add the remaining ¼ cup of almond milk, lemon juice, cayenne pepper, ketchup, ginger, salt, vinegar, and tofu and press the lid firmly in place.

- Blend on high speed for 1 minute.

- Pour into a clean jar and cover with a lid.

- Refrigerate for 1 hour or overnight. The dressing will keep for up to 1 week.

RANCHO DRESSING

(V) [VG]

Even if you don't live on a ranch, this is one versatile dressing, dipping sauce, and sandwich spread. Try it with Tempeh Nuggets (page 65). Don't be surprised if you keep dipping into it for just one more taste.

MAKES 1 CUP

4 to 5 sprigs flat-leaf parsley

1 cup vegan mayonnaise

½ cup unsweetened soy milk

1 tablespoon Dijon mustard

1 tablespoon white or apple cider vinegar

½ teaspoon salt

½ teaspoon garlic powder (not garlic salt)

½ teaspoon onion powder (not onion salt)

¼ teaspoon smoked paprika

On your mark . . .

- Wash the parsley, shake to remove any excess water, and dry by rolling in paper towels. Remove and discard the stems and coarsely chop the leaves.

Get set . . .

- Combine the parsley, mayonnaise, soy milk, mustard, vinegar, salt, garlic powder, onion powder, and paprika in a blender.

Blend!

- Press the lid firmly in place and blend at high speed for 1 minute or until smooth.

- Pour the dressing into a clean jar with a lid, cover, and refrigerate for 1 hour or overnight.

- Serve cold as a dipping sauce or salad dressing. The dressing will keep for up to 1 week.

RED COOL SLAW

(V) VG

Cooks' reputations can rise or fall by how good their slaw is! A cool, crunchy coleslaw with kale and red cabbage is sure to get noticed when tossed with TLC Dressing (page 96). Kale has been around for 2000 years and is packed with vitamins. Its mild-mannered taste is the perfect partner for its snappy cousin, red cabbage. Serve the slaw alongside Red, White, and Blue Cheese Potato Salad (page 93) or with The New Tempeh Burger (page 37).

SERVES 8 TO 10

5 to 6 purple or green kale leaves

1 small head red cabbage

4 scallions

2 plum tomatoes

½ cup TLC Dressing (page 96)

½ teaspoon celery seeds

1 teaspoon salt

½ teaspoon freshly ground black pepper

On your mark . . .

- Fill a clean sink with fresh cold water.

- Drop the kale leaves into the water. Let them soak for a few minutes, gently moving them around with your very clean hands to help dislodge any dirt. Lift up the leaves and put them in a colander to drain.

- Take one leaf at a time and lay it on a cutting board. Using the tip of a sharp knife, cut the stem out of the center. Discard the stem (or wrap and refrigerate it to save for another recipe). Stack the leaves in a separate pile. Continue until all the stems have been removed.

- Beginning at one end of the pile, tightly roll some of the leaves into a long cigar shape. Slice them crosswise into very thin strips, the thinner the better. This slicing technique is called *chiffonade*. Be patient, as this is a slow process. Place the strips in a bowl large enough to hold all the ingredients. Cut the remaining leaves and add to the bowl.

- Remove any dark or discolored leaves from the cabbage. Cut off and discard the stem from the bottom. Cut the cabbage in half and, using the tip of a sharp knife, cut out the white core and discard.

- Lay the cabbage cut side down on a cutting board. Slice into very thin slices, the thinner the better. Measure out about 4 cups and add the cut cabbage to the bowl with the kale.

Get set . . .

- Wash the scallions; cut off the root ends and any dark or discolored leaves. Cut into thin pieces, including 3 or 4 inches of the green tops. Combine with the kale-and-cabbage mixture. Toss well to combine.

- Wash the tomatoes and cut out the stem circle at the top. Cut the tomato into small chunks and add to the bowl.

Toss!

- Add the TLC Dressing, celery seeds, salt, and pepper to the bowl and toss well to combine all the ingredients.

- Cover and refrigerate for 1 hour or overnight.

- Toss well just before serving.

CHEF'S TIP

When shopping for kale, avoid bunches with limp leaves; look instead for deep, green or red, frilly leaves. If you're not using the kale right away, wrap and store it in the coldest part of the refrigerator.

Use within 3 to 4 days. Red cabbage tastes best with fresh-looking leaves and a head that feels heavy for its size. It will keep if well wrapped and refrigerated for up to 1 week.

Curly green kale

PASTA AND POLENTA PERFECTS

SPRING TABLE
PASTA • 104

THREE-CHEESE
POLENTA PIE • 107

INSTANT
POLENTA • 110

MAKE-A-SCENE
PASTA • 111

MAKE-A-SCENE
PASTA RAW
VERSION • 115

SPRING TABLE PASTA

Ⓥ VG

Bring spring to your table with this recipe even in the deepest days of winter. Have you ever pulled a carrot fresh out of the earth and after a quick rinse, taken a big bite? The flavor is . . . well . . . sweet like candy! Fresh picked vegetables right out of the ground are delectable delights. Whether you grow your own, hand pick them at the farmers' market, or carefully select them at the supermarket, vegetables are a superlative food. Everybody loves a cook that has a knack for preparing vegetables. Here is a show-off pasta that is spectacular to look at and has the appealing flavor of each of its fresh ingredients. What could be better than everyday vegetables turned into an extraordinary and exciting pasta?

SERVES 6

1 small red onion

2 cloves garlic

1 stalk celery

1 medium-size carrot, unpeeled

8 ounces red or green Swiss chard

1 pound fresh asparagus

1 pound fresh tomatoes

1 medium-size zucchini, unpeeled

1 small bunch fresh basil or
    1½ teaspoons dried

3 tablespoons extra-virgin olive oil

2 teaspoons salt

¼ teaspoon crushed red pepper flakes

Freshly ground black pepper to taste

½ cup Homemade Vegetable Stock
    (page 77) or canned low-sodium
    vegetable broth

½ teaspoon dried oregano

1 pound dried linguine or spaghetti

Freshly grated Parmigiano-Reggiano
    or vegan Parmesan, for passing at
    the table

On your mark, get set . . .

- Peel the red onion, chop into small pieces, and put into a large bowl.

- Slightly crush the garlic by laying the flat side of a chef's knife on the clove and pressing firmly to break open the skin. Remove the skin, cut off the root end, and discard. Finely chop the garlic and add to the onion.

- Wash and scrub the celery and carrot and chop into small pieces. Add to the bowl with the onion and garlic.

- Wash the Swiss chard stems with the leaves and cut into ½-inch pieces. Put in a medium bowl.

- Wash the asparagus in cold water, peel it with a vegetable peeler, and cut off the bottom few inches of the stalks. Cut the asparagus into 1-inch pieces and add to the bowl with the Swiss chard and asparagus.

- Wash the tomatoes and cut out the stem circles at the top. Dice the tomatoes into small chunks and add to the bowl with the other vegetables.

- Wash the zucchini, cut into 1-inch slices, and add to the bowl with the Swiss chard.

- Wash the basil to remove any sand or dirt, shake to remove excess water, and dry by rolling in paper towels. Remove the leaves from the stems, tear the leaves into small pieces, and set aside. Discard the stems.

Cook!

- Heat a 12- to 14-inch skillet over low heat for 30 seconds. Add the olive oil, red onion, garlic, celery, and carrot and sauté for 10 minutes.

- Add the Swiss chard, asparagus, tomatoes, zucchini, 2 teaspoons of salt, red pepper flakes, and black pepper. Carefully mix together all the ingredients and cook for 3 minutes, stirring frequently to prevent the vegetables from sticking.

- Add the vegetable stock, basil, and oregano.

- Bring the vegetables to a gentle boil, reduce the heat to low, and simmer, uncovered, for 20 minutes.

- While the sauce is simmering, cook the linguine or spaghetti according to the package directions.

- When the spaghetti is al dente, remove 1 cup of the cooking liquid and set aside. Drain the pasta in a colander. Pour the drained spaghetti into a large serving bowl.

- Spoon one ladle of the hot sauce over the spaghetti and mix well, coating all the strands with the sauce. Add the reserved pasta water. Pour the rest of the sauce over the pasta and toss to coat.

- Serve hot, passing the grated cheese at the table.

THREE-CHEESE POLENTA PIE

Ⓥ

Feel like you're in the mood for some real comfort food? Ready to indulge in a dish that's just a little excessive? Then here's what you've been craving. What makes it so tantalizing is the mushroom, tomato, and cheese filling baked and layered between sliced polenta. It will get everybody's attention when you bring it to the table.

SERVES 6 TO 8

1 pound assorted mushrooms (white, cremini, or baby portobello)

1 medium-size yellow onion

2 cloves garlic

3 plum tomatoes

4 to 5 basil leaves or 1 teaspoon dried

3 ounces fontina cheese

3 ounces mozzarella cheese

3 ounces Parmigiano-Reggiano cheese

⅓ cup whole milk

3 tablespoons extra-virgin olive oil

1½ teaspoons dried oregano

1½ teaspoons salt

½ teaspoon freshly ground black pepper

1 tablespoon butter

2 teaspoons cornstarch mixed with 1 tablespoon cold water

½ cup water

Instant Polenta (page 110)

On your mark . . .

- ▪ With a vegetable brush or paper towel, brush off any dirt from the mushrooms. Coarsely chop the mushrooms and set aside.

- ▪ Peel the onion, finely chop, and set aside.

- ▪ Slightly crush the garlic by laying the flat side of a chef's knife on the clove and pressing firmly to break open the skin. Remove the skin, cut off the root end, and discard. Coarsely chop and combine with the onion and set aside.

- ▪ Wash the tomatoes and cut out the stem circle on the top. Coarsely chop the tomatoes, add to a small bowl, and set aside.

- ▪ If you are using fresh basil leaves, wash and shake to remove the excess water and dry by rolling in paper towels. Tear into small pieces and set aside.

Get set . . .

- Using the largest holes of a four-sided grater, grate the fontina, mozzarella, and Parmigiano-Reggiano cheese and combine in a medium bowl. You should have a total of 1½ cups of grated cheese. Add the milk, mix well, and set aside.

Cook!

- Preheat the oven to 400°F with a rack in the middle of the oven.

- Heat the olive oil in a 12-inch skillet over medium heat for 30 seconds until hot but not smoking.

- Add the onion and garlic and sauté for 3 to 4 minutes, until translucent. If the onions or garlic start to brown, lower the heat.

- Add the chopped tomatoes, basil, oregano, salt, pepper, and butter. Cook for 3 to 4 minutes, until the tomatoes are tender.

- Mix the cornstarch and water and add to the tomato sauce, stirring to combine with all the ingredients.

- Add the chopped mushrooms and carefully mix all the ingredients together. Be careful not to spill the ingredients over the edge of the pan.

- Add the ½ cup water and mix well. Reduce the heat to low and cook at a gentle boil for 15 minutes or until most of the liquid has thickened. Stir occasionally to prevent sticking. If necessary, reduce the heat to low.

- Cut the polenta into long ¼- to ½-inch slices. Arrange them, so they cover the bottom and the sides of a 10-inch cast-iron skillet or baking dish. It is all right if some of the pan shows between the slices.

- Spoon one-half of the tomato mixture evenly over the slices. Then spoon one-half of the cheese-and-milk mixture over the tomato mixture.

- Cut another layer of polenta into ¼- to ½-inch slices and repeat the step above, ending with the cheese-and-milk mixture on top.

- Bake for 35 to 40 minutes, until the top is browned and bubbly.

- Let the pie cool for 20 minutes.

- Cut into slices and serve hot.

CHEF'S TIP

This pie can be made in advance, cooled, covered, and refrigerated. When you are ready to serve, reheat in a 350°F oven for 25 to 30 minutes, until heated through.

INSTANT POLENTA

Ⓥ VG

When you need to make a fast meal, polenta is kitchen gold. Once you experience Instant Polenta's versatility, it will become an all-time favorite.

SERVES 4

6½ cups water

1¼ teaspoons salt

2 tablespoons extra-virgin olive oil

2 cups instant polenta

On your mark, get set, cook!

- ◼ Combine the water, salt, and olive oil in a 6-quart pan with a lid. Bring to a boil over high heat.

- ◼ Slowly pour in the polenta and stir with a wooden spoon or a whisk to break up any lumps. Be careful that you don't splash yourself.

- ◼ Reduce the heat to low, cover the pan, and simmer for 10 minutes. Remove the lid and stir occasionally to prevent sticking.

- ◼ Rinse a 10-inch square or round glass or metal baking dish with cold water but don't dry it. Place it next to the stove.

- ◼ Carefully pour the cooked polenta into the wet baking dish. With a wet spoon or rubber spatula, smooth the surface of the hot polenta to even out the thickness.

- ◼ Let the polenta cool completely and become firm. It will take about 20 minutes.

- ◼ Once it is cool, it is ready to cut into slices for your recipe.

- ◼ Polenta can also be covered with plastic wrap and refrigerated. It will keep for up to 1 week.

MAKE-A-SCENE PASTA

(V) [VG]

How much does pasta have to suffer in salads or stand lost in countless bad combinations that are overcooked and abandoned on buffets? Most pasta salads are just too dreary to make a scene. Not this one, though. Here the ever-popular avocado combines into an Italian-style guacamole sauce that is over-the-top luscious, rich, and guaranteed to get noticed. Make-a-Scene Pasta is easy to prepare with whole-wheat pasta.

SERVES 4 TO 6

1 pound cherry or grape tomatoes (3 to 3½ cups)

6 to 8 scallions

20 fresh basil leaves

⅓ cup extra-virgin olive oil

1½ teaspoons salt

1 teaspoon freshly ground black pepper

8 ounces organic whole-wheat fusilli, penne, rotini, or spaghetti

2 ripe avocados

On your mark . . .

- ▣ Wash the cherry tomatoes and remove and discard any stems. Cut the tomatoes into quarters, put into a large bowl, and set aside.

- ▣ Wash the scallions. Remove the root ends and any dark or discolored leaves. Cut both the white part and 3 to 4 inches of the green tops into small pieces and add to the tomatoes. Toss to combine.

- ▣ Wash the basil, shake off any excess water, and wrap in a paper towel to dry. Tear the basil leaves into small pieces and add to scallions and tomatoes.

Get set . . .

- ▣ Add the olive oil, salt, and pepper to the bowl and toss well.

- ▣ Using the back of a metal spoon, lightly press the tomatoes to break them down and extract some of the juice. Toss again.

- ▣ Cover the bowl with a sheet of wax paper or plastic wrap and let it stand at room temperature.

Cook!

- Cook the pasta until al dente according to package directions.

- Drain the pasta in a colander. Add to the tomato mixture. Toss to combine.

- Lay an avocado on the cutting board. With the tip of a sharp knife, start at the stem end and cut lengthwise down the avocado and up the other side. Remember that there is a large pit inside, so don't try to cut through the flesh.

- Pick the avocado up and, holding it in both hands, twist it in opposite directions to separate the halves. Scoop out the pit with a tablespoon and discard. Scrape out the avocado pulp and cut into small chunks. Add it to the bowl with the tomato mixture.

- Repeat with the remaining avocado.

- Gently toss the salad until all the ingredients are combined.

- Arrange the salad on a serving platter.

- Serve warm or at room temperature.

MAKE-A-SCENE PASTA RAW VERSION

Ⓥ ⓋⒼ Ⓡ

Fresh zucchini noodles replace cooked pasta for this one-of-a-kind raw pasta dish.

SERVES 6

3 plump zucchini

1 pound cherry or grape tomatoes
   (3 to 3½ cups)

1 bunch scallions

20 fresh basil leaves

⅓ cup extra-virgin olive oil

1½ teaspoons salt

1 teaspoon freshly ground black
   pepper

2 ripe avocados

On your mark . . .

- Wash the zucchini. Leave the stems and tips on. Using a vegetable peeler, peel the outer skin of the zucchini to expose the white flesh underneath. Discard the outer skin. Dry the zucchini with paper towels. Cut off the bottoms. Using a vegetable peeler, slice off long ribbons from the white flesh. Try to keep the ribbons narrow. Slightly turn the zucchini after each peel.

- Continue peeling and turning the zucchini until you reach the center of the squash. Once the core of the zucchini is exposed and the orange colored rows of seeds are visible, you have peeled far enough. (Wrap and refrigerate any unpeeled zucchini core to save for vegetable stock.)

- Spread the zucchini noodles on a large baking sheet or platter and allow them to air dry while you prepare the sauce.

Get set . . .

- Wash the cherry tomatoes and remove and discard any stems. Cut the tomatoes in quarters, add to a large bowl, and set aside.

- Wash the scallions. Remove the root ends and any dark or discolored leaves. Cut both the white part and 3 to 4 inches of the green tops into small pieces and add to the tomatoes. Toss to combine.

- Wash the basil, shake off any excess water, and wrap in paper towels to dry.

Tear the basil leaves into small pieces and add to the bowl with the scallions and tomatoes.

■ Add the olive oil, salt, and pepper to the bowl and toss well.

■ Using the back of a metal spoon, lightly press the tomatoes to break them down and extract some of the juice. Toss again.

■ Cover the bowl with a sheet of wax paper or plastic wrap and let it stand at room temperature.

■ Lay the avocado on the cutting board. With the tip of a sharp knife, start at the stem end and cut lengthwise down the avocado and up the other side. Remember that there is a large pit inside, so don't try to cut through the flesh.

■ Pick the avocado up and, holding it in both hands, twist it in opposite directions to separate the halves. Scoop out the pit with a tablespoon and discard. Scrape out the avocado pulp and cut into small chunks. Add it to the bowl with the tomato mixture.

■ Repeat with the remaining avocado.

Toss!

■ Gently toss until all the ingredients are combined.

■ Add the zucchini noodles to the sauce and gently mix together.

■ Arrange the tossed pasta on a serving platter.

■ Serve warm or at room temperature.

BIG PLATES

CURRIED VEGETABLE
STIR-FRY • 120

SWEET-AND-SOUR
TOFU STIR-FRY • 123

RATATOUILLE • 125

EAT LOAF • 131

CHUNKY MUSHROOM
GRAVY • 134

HODGEPODGE • 137

SPINACH PIE • 141

PHYLLO DOUGH • 145

SWEET-AND-SOUR TOFU STIR-FRY

Ⓥ VG

This stir-fry is amazingly popular because it's easy to toss together once the tofu is marinated, and it looks downright tantalizing when you bring it to the table. Traditionlally the sour part of the recipe is vinegar, but here lemon juice adds a fresh accent to the finished dish. If you have a wok in your kitchen that you haven't used for a while, now is the time to get it wok-ing.

SERVES 4

MARINATED TOFU
8 ounces extra-firm tofu

1 lemon

2-inch piece fresh ginger

2 tablespoons ketchup, homemade (page 155) or store-bought

1 tablespoon tamari or soy sauce

1 tablespoon honey or agave nectar

1 small red bell pepper

2 ounces (1 medium-size) shiitake mushroom

½ cup bamboo shoots or hearts of palm

4 scallions

½ cup unsalted cashews

2 tablespoons peanut, safflower, or extra-virgin olive oil

On your mark . . .

- Drain the tofu in a colander for 2 to 3 minutes. Lay it on a cutting board and pat dry on both sides with paper towels. Cut the tofu into long strips and then into 2-inch cubes. Place in a small bowl.

- To make the marinade, cut the lemon in half, squeeze the juice through a small strainer to catch any seeds, and put the juice in a small bowl. (Wrap the other half of the lemon and refrigerate it to save for another recipe.)

- Peel and finely chop the ginger and add to the lemon juice.

- Add the ketchup, tamari, and honey. Mix well, pour the marinade over the tofu, and toss well to combine.

- Refrigerate for at least 30 minutes or overnight.

- Wash the tomatoes and cut out the stem circles at the top. Chop the tomatoes into medium-size chunks and set aside.

- Wash the parsley, shake to remove any excess water, and dry by rolling in paper towels. Pull the leaves from the stems, coarsely chop, and set aside. Discard the stems.

- Drain the eggplant in a colander.

- Lay a couple of sheets of paper towels on a counter. Place the eggplant, a handful at a time, on the paper towels. Lay another sheet of paper towels over them and gently pat dry. Wipe out the bowl with a paper towel and return the eggplant to the bowl.

- Repeat these steps with the zucchini.

Cook!

- Place a 2½-quart stovetop-safe casserole or heavy-bottomed pot with a lid next to the stove.

- In a 10- to 12-inch skillet or heavy-bottomed pan with a lid, heat 2 tablespoons of the olive oil over medium heat until hot but not smoking.

- Gently fry the eggplant for 2 minutes on each side or until just beginning to brown. Be careful not to break up the pieces. Transfer the eggplant to a clean plate.

- Heat another 2 tablespoons of the olive oil in the same pan over medium heat until hot but not smoking.

- Fry the zucchini for 2 minutes on each side or until just beginning to brown. Be careful not to break up the pieces. Transfer to a clean plate.

- Add the remaining 4 tablespoons of olive oil to the skillet and sauté the onion and peppers for 10 minutes or until they are soft. Stir occasionally to avoid sticking.

- Add the tomatoes, garlic, remaining ½ teaspoon salt, and pepper and cook for 5 to 7 minutes, until the tomatoes start to release their liquid. Turn off the heat.

- Spoon about one-third of the tomato mixture into the casserole dish.

- Layer one-third of the eggplant and one-third of the zucchini on top of the tomatoes.

- Sprinkle on a generous 1 tablespoon of the parsley.

- Layer one-third more of the tomato mixture, one-third more of the eggplant, and one-third more of the zucchini. Sprinkle on another generous 1 tablespoon of parsley.

▪ Layer the remaining vegetables on top, following the same steps, and finish with the remaining parsley.

▪ Cover the pan and bring to a simmer over low heat. Cook for 10 to 12 minutes or until the vegetables begin to release juice. If the pan is simmering too fast, lower the heat.

▪ Remove the lid and lift up one side of the pan to allow the juices to flow so you can baste the dish. You may have to move some of the vegetables aside.

▪ Raise the heat to medium-low. Cook, uncovered, for 12 to 15 minutes, until the vegetables are tender. Baste the vegetables occasionally as they simmer and continue to cook until almost all the liquid has evaporated.

▪ Serve hot or at room temperature.

CHEF'S TIP

This recipe takes a good deal of time so read it completely before you decide to make it. The reward is that ratatouille is the perfect recipe to use to show off fresh vegetables from your garden or that come from your farmers' market.

EAT LOAF

(V) VG

When some dishes bake, their aromas are so enticing that you count the minutes until it's time to take them out of the oven. Eat Loaf is one of those dishes. It is especially good when served with Chunky Mushroom Gravy (page 134). In the unlikely event there are leftovers, this dish makes an outrageously delicious sandwich.

SERVES 6

8 ounces baby portobello or cremini mushrooms

1 small onion

2 cloves garlic

1 14-ounce block extra-firm tofu

½ cup old fashioned rolled oats (not quick-cooking)

½ cup panko or plain bread crumbs

¾ cup toasted wheat germ

1 carrot

1 celery stalk

1 small red or yellow bell pepper

5 to 6 sprigs flat-leaf parsley

1 10-ounce can Ro*tel brand diced tomatoes and green chiles

4 tablespoons extra-virgin olive oil

1 tablespoon smoked paprika

1 teaspoon salt

½ teaspoon freshly ground black pepper

½ cup grated Parmesan cheese or vegan Parmesan cheese

Chunky Mushroom Gravy (page 134) heated

On your mark . . .

- ▪ Lightly oil a 9-inch loaf pan and set aside.

- ▪ Using a vegetable brush or paper towel, brush off any dirt from the mushrooms. Don't wash them or they will absorb too much water and become soggy.

- ▪ Coarsely chop the mushrooms into medium-size chunks and set aside.

- ▪ Peel and finely chop the onion, measure ½ cup, and set aside.

- ▪ Slightly crush the garlic by laying the flat side of a chef's knife on the clove and pressing firmly to break open the skin. Peel and finely chop the garlic, combine with the onions, and set aside.

Get set . . .

- Drain the tofu in a colander.

- In a large bowl combine the oats, bread crumbs, and wheat germ and set aside.

- Wash and peel the carrot. Cut into small chunks, measure out ½ cup, and add to a medium-size bowl.

- Wash the celery and cut into small chunks, measure ½ cup, and add to the carrots.

- Wash the bell pepper and cut out the stem at the top. Cut in half and remove and discard the seeds and white veins. Coarsely chop the pepper, measure ½ cup, and add to the carrots and celery.

- Wash the parsley, shake to remove any excess water, and dry by rolling in paper towels. Coarsely chop and add to the bowl with the vegetables.

- Toss well to combine the ingredients and set aside.

- Drain the tomatoes and chiles through a fine-mesh strainer over the sink and set aside.

Cook!

- Preheat the oven to 375°F with a rack in the middle of the oven.

- In a 10½-inch skillet, heat 2½ tablespoons of the olive oil over medium heat for about 30 seconds, until hot but not smoking. Add the onions and garlic and sauté for 2 to 3 minutes, or until the onions are soft and translucent.

- Add the vegetable combination and smoked paprika and sauté for 4 to 5 minutes, until the vegetables are tender.

- Add the mushrooms, salt, pepper, and 1 tablespoon of the olive oil. Crumble the tofu into the pan and mix well to combine all the ingredients.

- Add the drained tomato-and-chile mixture. Combine the ingredients. Be careful to avoid spilling over the sides of the pan.

- Cover the pan with the lid slightly ajar, lower the heat, and simmer for 10 minutes. Turn off the burner and let cool for 15 minutes.

- Add the sautéed vegetables-and-tofu mixture to the bowl with the oat mixture.

- Add the cheese and mix well to moisten all the ingredients.

- Spoon the mixture into the prepared loaf pan and, using the back of a large spoon, press to pack firmly.

- Brush the top of the loaf with the remaining olive oil.

- Place on the middle rack of the oven and bake for 60 to 65 minutes, until firm to the touch and browned.

- Let the loaf cool for 10 to 15 minutes.

- Carefully invert the loaf pan onto a serving dish.

- Cut into slices and serve hot with the gravy.

CHUNKY MUSHROOM GRAVY

Ⓥ VG

What good is a great Eat Loaf without the best possible gravy to go along with it? When you're craving that enticing aroma and rich flavor that only tasty gravy can satisfy, this is the recipe for you. Try it and discover why everyone at your table is going to say, "Pass the gravy!"

SERVES 6

12 ounces baby portobello, cremini, or white mushrooms

1 small white or yellow onion

2½ tablespoons butter or vegan margarine

¼ cup unbleached all-purpose flour

3 cups Homemade Vegetable Stock (page 77) or canned low-sodium vegetable broth

1 tablespoon tamari or soy sauce

1½ teaspoons poultry seasoning

½ teaspoon salt

¼ teaspoon freshly ground black pepper

On your mark, get set . . .

- ▪ Using a vegetable brush or paper towel, brush off any dirt from the mushrooms. Don't wash them or they will absorb too much of water and become soggy.

- ▪ Coarsely chop the mushrooms into medium-size chunks and set aside.

- ▪ Peel and chop the onion into small chunks and set aside.

Cook!

- ▪ Melt the butter in a 10½-inch skillet over medium heat.

- ▪ Add the onion and sauté for 2 minutes or until soft and translucent.

- ▪ Add the mushrooms and sauté for 3 minutes or until soft and just starting to brown.

- Add the flour and stir well to coat the mushroom-onion mixture. Cook, stirring frequently, for 2 minutes. Pour in 1 cup of the vegetable stock and mix until slightly thickened.

- Bring the gravy to a simmer and continue to stir to prevent lumps. Cook for 1 minute until thickened.

- Add the remaining 2 cups of stock and tamari or soy sauce. Stir well until smooth.

- Add the poultry seasoning, salt, and pepper.

- Reduce the heat to low and simmer, uncovered, for 10 minutes. Stir frequently to prevent sticking or lumping. If the gravy is too thick, thin with a little water or vegetable stock. Skim off any foam or impurities that rise to the top.

- Pour into a gravy boat and serve hot.

HODGEPODGE

(V) VG

It's a cloudy, cold winter afternoon and you want something home cooked. You have a little of this and some of that and are wondering how to bring it all together into something tasty. Try this creamy mix of protein-packed quinoa and lentils simmered with aromatic Indian spices, chiles, and fresh ginger. Even if the sun is shining, any day is the right day for a Hodgepodge.

SERVES 4 TO 6

⅔ cup rinsed quinoa

⅔ cup red, yellow, or brown lentils

1 serrano or jalapeño chile

1-inch piece fresh ginger

2 tablespoons safflower oil, canola oil, butter, or vegan margarine

½ teaspoon yellow mustard seeds

½ teaspoon fennel seeds

¼ teaspoon ground turmeric

1 teaspoon salt

2 cups water

On your mark . . .

- ■ Pour the quinoa into a fine-mesh strainer and rinse well with cold water.

- ■ Combine the quinoa and lentils in a large bowl. Fill the bowl with cold water and soak for 30 minutes.

- ■ Drain through a fine-mesh strainer.

Get set . . .

- ■ Slip on a pair of latex kitchen gloves. Remove the stems from the chile and cut in half lengthwise. Rinse under cold water. Scrape out the seeds with the tip of a teaspoon and discard. Chop into small dice and set aside. Rinse, dry, and remove the gloves.

- ■ Peel the outer skin from the ginger and discard. Cut the ginger into thin slices. Stack the slices on top of each other and cut them into long strips. Finely chop or mince the ginger strips into tiny pieces and set aside.

Cook!

- Heat the oil or butter in a 4- to 5-quart saucepan over medium-low heat for 30 to 40 seconds or until hot but not smoking.

- Add the mustard and fennel seeds.

- Cook the seeds, stirring constantly, for about 2 minutes or until they darken.

- Add the chile, ginger, and turmeric. Cook for 1 minute.

- Add the quinoa, lentils, and salt.

- Stir well to combine all the ingredients and cook, uncovered, for 1 minute. Stir to prevent sticking.

- Add the water, stir once, and bring to a boil. This will take 4 to 5 minutes.

- Cover the pan and lower the heat to simmer. Cook for 15 minutes.

- Turn off the heat and let the pan rest undisturbed for 5 minutes.

- When you are ready to serve, remove the cover and fluff the Hodgepodge with a fork.

- Serve hot.

The photograph of Hodgepodge on page 136 shows it in a traditional Indian lunch box. The stacked metal containers are perfect for transporting a delicious lunch to travelers, students, and office workers.

Fresh ginger

SPINACH PIE

(V)

A flavorful spinach, leek, and feta cheese filling baked in a flaky phyllo crust is one of the most beloved of all dishes. It is popular in diners all across the country, but when you make it in your own kitchen, you will taste real spinach pie. Spend the extra time to make this pie from scratch, and you'll taste why it has such a following of devoted food lovers. Shop for Greek feta, available in most supermarkets, to add the authentic taste this dish demands.

SERVES 12

1½ pounds fresh spinach

4 scallions

1 small bunch flat-leaf parsley (about 10 stems)

1 small bunch fresh dill

1 small bunch fresh mint

2 leeks

¼ cup extra-virgin olive oil

½ cup (1 stick) unsalted butter

¼ teaspoon salt

8 ounces feta cheese

3 large eggs, beaten

1 package (20 sheets) Phyllo Dough (page 145), completely thawed

On your mark . . .

- [ ] Fill a clean sink with cold water. Separate the leaves of the spinach and drop them into the water.

- [ ] Let them soak for a few minutes, gently moving them around with your very clean hands to help dislodge any dirt.

- [ ] Carefully lift the spinach out of the water and put into a colander, being careful not to disturb the water too much.

- [ ] Drain the water from the sink and clean any dirt or sand from the bottom. Refill the sink with cold water and repeat the washing at least once.

- [ ] If there is still sand or dirt in the sink, repeat a final time.

- [ ] Drain the spinach. Shake the colander to remove any excess water. Coarsely chop the spinach and return to the colander to continue to drain.

Get set . . .

- Wash and trim the scallions. Cut off the root ends and discard. Finely chop the white bottoms and 3 to 4 inches of the green stems and set aside.

- Wash the parsley, shake to remove any excess water, and dry by rolling in paper towels. Coarsely chop and set aside.

- Wash the dill and mint and shake off any excess water. Remove the mint leaves, discard the stems, and dry the leaves by rolling them with the dill in paper towels. Chop the mint and dill together and set aside.

- Cut off the root ends of the leeks and discard any brown or damaged leaves. Place the leeks on a cutting board and, using the tip of a sharp knife, slice the leeks in half lengthwise. Wash under cold water, spreading the leaves apart with your fingers to separate the layers. Rinse out any sand that may be trapped. Repeat with the other halves. Slice the white section and about 1 inch of the pale green section into thin slices and set aside.

Cook!

- Preheat the oven to 350°F with a rack in the middle of the oven.

- Combine the olive oil and 2 tablespoons of butter in a 3-quart saucepan. Heat over low heat for 30 seconds. Add the leeks and scallions and sauté for 5 to 7 minutes until tender.

- Add the drained spinach and salt and sauté for another 5 to 7 minutes or until the spinach is wilted.

- Pour the cooked spinach mixture into a colander to drain. Using the back of a large spoon, gently press on the spinach to extract liquid. Let the spinach mixture drain for 10 to 15 minutes.

- In a large bowl, combine the feta, eggs, parsley, dill, and mint. Add the drained spinach mixture. Mix well to combine all the ingredients and set aside. This is the pie filling.

- Generously butter the bottom and sides of a 9- by 13-inch baking dish.

- Remove the phyllo from the refrigerator and divide the sheets into two even stacks. There should be ten sheets in each stack. Cover the stacks with a damp cloth or plastic wrap to prevent drying.

- Melt the remaining 6 tablespoons butter in a saucepan over low heat and place the saucepan on your work surface.

- Carefully lift one sheet and place it in the baking dish.

- Immediately cover the remaining sheets with a damp cloth or a sheet of plastic wrap to prevent drying out.

- Lightly dip tip of a pastry brush into the melted butter and brush the sheet with a little butter. Make sure to brush the surface of the sheet all the way to the edges. It is okay to be messy. If the edges are larger than the pan, tuck them in with the brush as you spread the melted butter. Repeat this step with nine more sheets to create the bottom crust of the pie.

- Spread the spinach filling evenly over the buttered sheets.

- Repeat the buttering and layering step with the other 10 sheets of phyllo to create the top crust of the pie. Tuck in the edges.

- Using the tip of a sharp knife, score the pie into 12 pieces. Your knife should cut down just to the filling.

- Bake for 40 to 45 minutes, until the top is golden brown and crispy. Let cool for 15 minutes.

- To serve, use a sharp knife to cut through each serving by following the scored lines on the top crust of the pie.

- Spinach pie can be served hot, at room temperature, or cold.

PHYLLO DOUGH

Many cooks avoid phyllo dough, the flaky and delicate Greek pastry, because they think it's too difficult to work with. If you follow some simple guidelines, phyllo dough is a great pastry and, in fact, is forgiving, even to rough handling. You can find it frozen in most supermarkets. Here are some basic rules to help ensure a successful phyllo baking experience:

- Read the phyllo package instructions and follow the thawing guidelines.
- Phyllo dries out quickly, so keep it covered with a damp cloth or plastic wrap on your work surface.
- Each sheet gets brushed with butter, oil, or a combination of both after it goes into your baking pan.

AND ON THE SIDE

CRISPY CUCUMBER
AND CARROT
PICKLES • 149

CUCUMBER AND
RADISH RELISH • 151

KETCHUP • 155

SALSA VERDE • 157

CARROT AND MINT
CHUTNEY • 161

CRISPY CUCUMBER AND CARROT PICKLES

Ⓥ VG

Preserving and canning fresh fruits, vegetables, and sauces is becoming incredibly popular with home cooks again. Making your own pickles, jams, and condiments is rewarding. Here are some recipes to whet your appetite. Traditional canning involves sterilized jars, precise timing, and careful monitoring of your ingredients. You might not want to go to all that trouble. These recipes, however, are simple and will get you started. If crunch is your thing, and crispy keeps you content, then these sweet-and-sour pickles are calling your name.

SERVES 6

1 red bell pepper

3 scallions

1 large cucumber

1 to 2 medium carrots

1 to 2 red or green jalapeño chiles

1 cup rice vinegar or white vinegar

1 cup water

1 cup firmly packed raw (turbinado) or light brown sugar

2 tablespoons salt

On your mark, get set . . .

- Wash the red bell pepper and cut out the stem at the top. Slice the pepper in half and remove the seeds and the white veins from the inside. Chop the pepper into medium-size pieces and transfer to a medium-size bowl.

- Wash the scallions, cut off the root ends, and discard any dark or discolored leaves. Finely chop into ¼-inch pieces, including 3 or 4 inches of the green tops, and add to the bell pepper.

- Peel the cucumber and cut in half lengthwise. Lay the cucumber, flat side down, on a cutting board and cut into ¼-inch slices, and add to the vegetable mixture.

- Wash and peel the carrots. Slice into thin circles and add to the rest of the vegetables.

- Slip on a pair of latex kitchen gloves. Remove the stem and cut the jalapeño in half lengthwise. Scrape out the seeds with the tip of a teaspoon and discard. Cut the chiles into thin slices and add to the bowl. Rinse, dry, and remove the gloves.

Cook!

■ In a medium saucepan, combine the vinegar, water, sugar, and salt. Bring the pan to a boil over medium-high heat. Cook for 2 to 3 more minutes at a medium boil or until the sugar is dissolved. Remove from the heat. This is the pickling syrup. Cool for 20 minutes at room temperature.

■ Pour the pickling syrup over the vegetables and stir well. Let the vegetables sit for 30 minutes or overnight before serving. The longer the vegetables sit, the hotter they will become.

■ To store the pickled vegetables, pack them in clean jars with the pickling syrup and cover with lids. Pickles will keep in the refrigerator for up to 2 weeks.

CHEF'S TIP

Make sure the jars and lids you are using for storing your finished pickles are spotlessly clean. You can accomplish this by putting them through a full cycle in the dishwasher before using.

CUCUMBER AND RADISH RELISH

Ⓥ VG

This relish is not only beautiful to look at, but it has a pleasing, zingy taste. Try it as a topper on sandwiches, serve it with sushi (page 55), or spoon it on The New Tempeh Burger (page 37).

SERVES 6

1 medium-size cucumber

6 red radishes

3 shallots

1-inch piece fresh ginger

3 to 4 sprigs cilantro

1 red or green jalapeño chile

¼ cup coconut vinegar or white vinegar

¼ cup water

¼ cup firmly packed raw (turbinado) or light brown sugar

½ teaspoon salt

On your mark, get set . . .

- Peel the cucumber and cut it in half lengthwise. Lay the cucumber, flat side down, on a cutting board and cut into ¼-inch slices. Finely chop the slices and put in a medium-size bowl.

- Wash the radishes, cut off the stem ends and root tips and discard. Cut the radishes in half, finely chop, and add to the bowl with the cucumbers.

- Cut the tops off the shallots and peel off the skins. Cut the shallots into thin slices and add to the bowl with the cucumbers.

- Crush the ginger with the flat side of a knife. Remove the skin and discard. Finely chop and add to the bowl with the vegetables.

- Wash the cilantro and shake off the excess water. Pull off the leaves and discard the stems. Wrap the leaves in a paper towel to dry. Coarsely chop and add to the bowl.

- Slip on a pair of latex kitchen gloves. Remove the stem and cut the chile in half. Rinse the chile under cold water. Scrape out the seeds with the tip of a teaspoon and discard. Cut the chile into thin slices and add to the bowl. Rinse, dry, and remove the gloves.

Cook!

- In a small saucepan, combine the vinegar, water, sugar, and salt.

- Bring to a boil over medium-high heat and stir occasionally to dissolve the sugar.

- Cook for 2 to 3 minutes at a medium boil or until the sugar and salt are dissolved. Remove from the heat and let cool for 10 minutes. This is the pickling syrup.

- Pour the pickling syrup over the vegetable mixture and stir well.

- Let the relish sit for 30 minutes at room temperature or cover and refrigerate overnight. The longer the relish sits, the hotter it will become.

- Toss well and serve cold or at room temperature. The relish will keep for 1 week, covered and refrigerated.

CHEF'S TIP

When storing your finished relish, make sure the jars and lids you are using are spotlessly clean. You can accomplish this by putting them through a full cycle in the dishwasher before using.

KETCHUP

Ⓥ VG

Ketchup was originally a Chinese sauce called *kêtsiap*. It was not thick or sweet, and it originally contained anchovies. Luckily for us, in 1869 in Sharpsburg, Pennsylvania, Henry J. Heinz added tomatoes to a recipe he had been developing. With the tomato as the key ingredient, Americans fell in love, and the rest is ketchup history. We consume almost 10 billion ounces (that's three bottles per person) a year. We all know it, we love it, and it's about time to give this most common condiment an uncommon makeover with a simple recipe. This ketchup is all dressed up with lots of places to go. You can use it on anything in place of the bottled version—and it comes straight from your own kitchen!

MAKES 3 CUPS

1 red bell pepper

1 small red onion

2-inch piece fresh ginger

1 28-ounce can chopped plum tomatoes

¼ cup rice vinegar or apple cider vinegar

1 cup firmly packed raw (turbinado) or light brown sugar

½ teaspoon ground allspice

¼ teaspoon cayenne pepper (optional)

½ cup chopped dates

1 teaspoon salt

On your mark . . .

- ■ Wash the bell pepper and cut out the stem on top. Cut in half and remove the seeds and white veins inside. Chop into small dice and put into a heavy-bottom pan large enough to hold all the ingredients.

- ■ Peel and chop the onion and add to the peppers.

- ■ Crush the ginger with the flat side of a knife. Remove the skin and discard. Finely chop the ginger and add to the onion and peppers.

Get set . . .

- ■ Add the tomatoes and their liquid, vinegar, sugar, allspice, cayenne, if using, dates, and salt.

- ■ Stir well to combine all the ingredients.

Cook!

- Bring to a boil over medium heat.

- Decrease the heat to low and simmer for 1¼ hours or until the mixture becomes thickened and is reduced by half. Stir occasionally to prevent sticking.

- Let cool completely.

- Divide the finished ketchup in half. Pour one half into a blender. Press the lid firmly in place and blend at high speed for 20 to 30 seconds until smooth.

- Repeat with the remaining ketchup.

- Pour the blended ketchup into a clean jar, seal tightly, refrigerate, and use within 1 week.

CHEF'S TIP

Make sure the jars and lids you use for storing your finished ketchup are spotlessly clean. You can accomplish this by putting them through a full cycle in the dishwasher before using.

SALSA VERDE

(V) VG

Authentic salsa verde made in your kitchen will far outshine any bottled version you will find in the supermarket. The blending of fresh tomatillos (page 67) cooked with onions, cilantro, and jalapeño creates one of the most exciting combinations in all of Mexican cooking. Just give it try and see for yourself.

SERVES 6

2 cloves garlic

½ small white onion

1 pound tomatillos

8 to 10 sprigs cilantro

1 to 2 jalapeño chiles

3 cups water

2 teaspoons salt

1 tablespoon safflower, corn, or canola oil

On your mark . . .

- Peel the garlic and leave whole.

- Peel the onion. Chop into small pieces and set aside.

- Peel off the papery husks from the tomatillos and discard. Wash the tomatillos with cold water and set aside.

- Wash the cilantro, shake to remove excess water, dry by rolling in paper towels, and set aside.

- Wash the jalapeños and set aside.

Get set . . .

- Combine the water, salt, garlic cloves, tomatillos, and whole jalapeños in a 3-quart saucepan.

- Bring the water to a boil over medium-high heat. Decrease the heat to low and simmer, uncovered, for 10 minutes.

- Drain the mixture in a colander, reserving ½ cup of the cooking liquid in a small bowl. Transfer the tomatillo mixture, cilantro, and reserved cooking liquid to the jar of a blender.

- Press the lid almost completely in place, leaving it slightly ajar. Blend at low speed for a few seconds. Now press the lid firmly in place and blend at high speed for 10 to 15 seconds, until liquefied.

▢ Remove the jar from the blender and set near the stove.

Cook!

▢ Heat the oil in a 10-inch heavy-bottomed frying pan or cast-iron skillet over medium heat for about 30 seconds.

▢ Add the chopped onion. Cook for 4 to 5 minutes, until the onion becomes soft and translucent.

▢ Remove the pan from the heat and pour in the mixture from the blender. Have a lid close by, as the mixture will bubble and boil when it hits the hot pan. Cover the pan with the lid to prevent spattering.

▢ Remove the cover and cook on low heat for about 5 minutes, stirring occasionally.

▢ Let cool completely and serve.

Jalapeño peppers

CARROT AND MINT CHUTNEY

Ⓥ VG

Chutneys are a sweet-heat combo condiment that jazzes up anything you serve them with—especially something like Curried Vegetable Stir-Fry (page 120). You can also try this combination of carrots and mint as a crunchy, colorful mini-salad.

SERVES 4 TO 6

1 pound carrots

½ cup firmly packed raw (turbinado) or light brown sugar or agave nectar

½ cup rice vinegar or white vinegar

¼ teaspoon cayenne pepper

½ teaspoon curry powder

½ teaspoon salt

2 tablespoons safflower or canola oil

1-inch piece fresh ginger

3 to 4 sprigs fresh mint

½ cup shredded unsweetened coconut

On your mark . . .

- Wash and peel the carrots. Using the largest holes of a four-sided grater, grate the carrots into a large bowl.

- Combine the sugar, vinegar, cayenne, curry powder, salt, and oil in a small bowl. Mix well to dissolve the sugar. Add to the carrots and mix well to combine.

- Crush the ginger with the flat side of a knife. Remove the skin and discard. Finely chop the ginger and add it to the bowl with the carrots.

- Wash the mint and shake to remove any excess water. Pull off the leaves and discard the stems. Wrap the leaves in paper towels to dry. Coarsely chop and set aside.

Get set . . .

- Transfer the carrot mixture to a medium saucepan.

Cook!

- Bring to a gentle boil over medium heat and simmer for 4 minutes.

- Transfer the chutney to a bowl and add the chopped mint and unsweetened coconut. Toss well to combine.

- Serve immediately.

- Carrot chutney will keep for up to 1 week, covered and refrigerated.

CHEF'S TIP

To make the chutney raw, omit the steps under Cook! and add the chopped mint and unsweetened coconut to the other ingredients. Toss all the ingredients together and serve.

Sweet bell peppers

JUST DESSERTS

CHOCOLATE
CUPCAKES • 167

■

CHOCOLATE CREAM
FROSTING • 170

■

VANILLA
FROSTING • 171

■

VANILLA
CUPCAKES • 173

■

SNAPPY GINGER
COOKIES • 177

■

BLUEBERRY AND
DRIED CHERRY
CRUMBLE • 179

CHOCOLATE CUPCAKES
(V) VG

Cupcakes are superstars: rich, beautiful, luscious, and individual. Once you put your creative genius to work by topping each cupcake with frosting and tiny candies or sprinkles, they're ready for the spotlight on your table. According to culinary history, the cupcake probably originated in New England and was first mentioned in an 1869 American cookbook. Here it is all over again and just as welcome. Hello, cupcake!

MAKES 12

1 cup unbleached flour

½ cup dark or regular cocoa powder

¾ teaspoon baking soda

½ teaspoon baking powder

¼ teaspoon salt

1 cup unsweetened coconut milk

1 teaspoon white or apple cider vinegar

¾ cup firmly packed raw (turbinado) or light brown sugar

⅓ cup canola oil

1½ teaspoons pure vanilla extract

On your mark . . .

- Preheat the oven to 350°F with a rack in the middle of the oven.

- Line a 12-cup muffin pan with paper or foil liners and set aside.

Get set . . .

- Sift the flour, cocoa powder, baking soda, baking powder, and salt into a large bowl and set aside.

- Combine the coconut milk and the vinegar in a blender and let it stand for a few minutes or until the surface is lightly foaming.

- Add the sugar, oil, and vanilla to the blender. With the lid pressed firmly in place, blend at high speed for 30 seconds.

- Pour ½ of the wet mixture from the blender into the bowl of dry ingredients and mix with a rubber spatula or wooden spoon.

- Add the remaining wet mixture and stir well into an almost lump-free batter.

Cook!

- Using a standard-size ice cream scoop with a lever release, scoop up the batter. When the bowl of the ice cream scoop is about three-quarters full, pull the lever and drop the batter into each cup. The batter should fill the cup a little more than half full. Repeat with the rest of the batter.

- Bake for 18 to 20 minutes, until a wooden skewer inserted into the middle of a cupcake comes out with only a little batter on it.

- Place the whole pan of cupcakes on a wire cooling rack and cool completely.

CHEF'S TIP

Make sure to not overfill the baking cups with batter. You will need room to frost the finished cupcake.

CHOCOLATE CREAM FROSTING

(V) VG

The real fun starts when it's time to frost a cooled cupcake. The decorations can be understated, traditional, or totally outrageous. It is up to you. This chocolate frosting is rich and delicate and the perfect spreadable topper to transform your cupcakes into megastars.

MAKES ABOUT 1 CUP OR ENOUGH FOR 1 BATCH OF CUPCAKES

¼ cup vegan margarine

¼ cup non-hydrogenated vegetable shortening

2 cups confectioners' sugar

½ cup dark cocoa powder

3 tablespoons unsweetened coconut milk

1½ teaspoons pure vanilla extract

On your mark . . . get set . . . whip!

- Put the margarine and shortening in a medium bowl. Using an electric hand mixer, beat on medium speed for 1 minute or until smooth and fluffy.

- Combine the confectioners' sugar and cocoa powder in a flour sifter or fine-mesh hand strainer and sift or gently tap the sides to sift the ingredients into the bowl.

- Using an electric hand mixer, beat on medium speed until well combined.

- Add 2 tablespoons of the coconut milk and beat until smooth. Add the remaining 1 tablespoon of coconut milk and beat until well combined.

- Add the vanilla and beat until just combined.

- With a thin knife, spread the frosting at room temperature. Hold the cupcake with one hand and frost it with the other.

- You may also cover the frosting and refrigerate or freeze it for up to 2 months. Return to room temperature before spreading.

CHEF'S TIP

For a professional look, use a pastry bag and tips to pipe the frosting onto your cupcakes. Follow the instructions included with your pastry bag. If you don't have a pastry bag, use a plastic sandwich bag with 1/4-inch cut away from one of the bottom corners. Don't forget the sprinkles!

VANILLA FROSTING

Ⓥ VG

Spread this elegant, creamy frosting either on vanilla or chocolate cupcakes. It's a perfect frosting to dress up any cupcake and make it a work of kitchen art.

MAKES ABOUT 1 CUP OR ENOUGH FOR 1 BATCH OF CUPCAKES

¼ cup vegan margarine

¼ cup non-hydrogenated vegetable shortening

2½ cups confectioners' sugar

1½ teaspoons pure vanilla extract

3 tablespoons unsweetened coconut milk

On your mark . . . get set . . . whip!

- Put the margarine and shortening in a medium bowl. Using an electric hand mixer, beat on medium speed for 1 minute or until smooth and fluffy.

- Put the confectioners' sugar in a flour sifter or fine-mesh hand strainer and sift or gently tap the sides to sift the ingredients into the bowl.

- Add the vanilla and coconut milk and beat for another 2 minutes with the electric hand mixer.

- With a thin knife, spread the frosting at room temperature. Hold the cupcake with one hand and frost it with the other.

- You may also cover the frosting and refrigerate or freeze it for up to 2 months. Return to room temperature before spreading.

> **CHEF'S TIP**
>
> For a professional look, use a pastry bag and tips to pipe the frosting onto your cupcakes. Follow the instructions included with your pastry bag. If you don't have a pastry bag, use a plastic sandwich bag with ¼-inch cut away from one of the bottom corners. Don't forget the sprinkles!

VANILLA CUPCAKES

VG

Where would we be without the vanilla cupcake? Though a little shyer than its outspoken chocolate cousin, the vanilla cupcake is certainly no less luscious. It is just the right moist and delicate cake to show off your frosting and decorations. And who doesn't love to be surprised by a cupcake with a candle burning in the center? It's the perfect edible gift.

MAKES 12

1½ cups unbleached flour

¾ teaspoon baking soda

½ teaspoon baking powder

½ teaspoon salt

1¼ cups unsweetened coconut milk

1 teaspoon white vinegar

¾ cup firmly packed raw (turbinado) or light brown sugar

⅓ cup canola oil

2¼ teaspoons pure vanilla extract

On your mark . . .

- Preheat the oven to 350°F with a rack in the middle of the oven.
- Line a 12-cup muffin pan with paper or foil liners and set aside.

Get set . . .

- Sift the flour, baking soda, baking powder, and salt into a large bowl and set aside.
- Combine the coconut milk and the vinegar in a blender and let it stand for a few minutes or until the surface is lightly foaming.
- Add the sugar, oil, and vanilla to the blender. With the lid pressed firmly in place, blend at high speed for 30 seconds.
- Pour ½ of the wet mixture from the blender into the bowl of dry ingredients and mix with a rubber spatula or wooden spoon.
- Add the remaining wet mixture and stir well into an almost lump-free batter.

Cook!

- Using a standard-size ice cream scoop with a lever release, scoop up the batter. When the bowl of the ice cream scoop is about three-quarters full, pull the lever and drop the batter into each cup. The batter should fill the cup a little more than half full. Repeat with the rest of the batter.

■ Bake for 18 to 20 minutes or until a wooden skewer inserted into the middle of a cupcake comes out with only a little batter on it.

■ Place the whole pan of cupcakes on a wire cooling rack and cool completely.

BLUEBERRY AND DRIED CHERRY CRUMBLE

Ⓥ VG

This showy, easy-to-make fruit dessert has lots of different names and ways to prepare it, depending on where you live. Is it a buckle, crisp, pan dowdy, brown Betty, zonker, slump, cobbler, or a grunt? Think of it as a lazy cook's pie. Here fresh blueberries and dried cherries make the luscious filling, topped with a tender, golden brown crust of oats and nuts. Follow the recipe as written to keep it vegetarian, or substitute vegan margarine for the butter to make it vegan. Either way, it will make your heart crumble.

SERVES 8

4 cups (2 pints) fresh blueberries

½ cup dried cherries or cranberries

¼ cup instant tapioca

1 tablespoon orange juice

¾ cup old-fashioned rolled oats (not instant)

½ cup pecans, almonds, or walnuts

¾ cup whole-wheat flour

1 teaspoon ground cinnamon

½ teaspoon ground ginger

½ teaspoon salt

⅔ cup raw (turbinado) or light brown sugar

⅓ cup granulated sugar

½ cup (1 stick) plus 2 tablespoons unsalted butter or vegan margarine, at room temperature

Whipped cream, frozen yogurt, or nondairy whipped topping of your choice

On your mark . . .

- ■ Preheat the oven to 350°F with a rack in the middle of the oven. Place a foil-lined baking sheet on the rack below to catch any drips from the baking.

- ■ Pour the blueberries into a colander, look them over carefully, and remove any stems or berries that are shriveled.

- ■ Wash the berries with cold water and shake off the excess moisture.

- ■ Pour the blueberries and the dried cherries into a 10-inch ungreased pie dish or 10-inch baking pan. Sprinkle on the tapioca and the orange juice and toss well with a spoon. Set the berries aside for 15 minutes.

Get set . . .

- Fit a food processor with the all-purpose blade. Combine the oats, nuts, flour, cinnamon, ginger, salt, sugars, and butter in the food processor.

- Snap the lid in place and pulse 10 to 12 times, until the ingredients are crumbly.

- Spread the crumble on top of the berries, covering them completely. Use the back of a spoon to gently compact the crumble mixture to create a crust.

Cook!

- Bake for 45 to 50 minutes, until the top is lightly browned. Let cool for 20 minutes.

- Serve warm, topped with your choice of whipped cream, frozen yogurt, or nondairy whipped topping of your choice.

KITCHEN
ESSENTIALS

■ ■ ■ ■ ■ ■ ■ ■ ■ ■ ■

Agave nectar or agave syrup

Agave nectar is produced from the blue agave cactus, more commonly called the century plant. The cactus grows in the hot, dry regions of Mexico and the southwestern United States. The nectar is extracted from the spiked leaves of the cactus and has a sweetness similar to honey but not as thick. It is a popular alternative sweetener to honey in vegan recipes.

Allspice

These dried berries are from Jamaica and are available whole or ground. If you have a spice grinder, buy the berries whole and grind them yourself for maximum flavor.

Almond milk

Almond milk is made by blending ground almonds with water into a thick liquid from which the milk is strained and extracted. Its flavor is somewhat sweet with a hint of nuttiness. Almond milk is a popular alternative to cow's milk and soy milk, and it's used in vegan, raw, and vegetarian recipes. It is high in protein and calcium. It's lower in calories than cow's milk and contains no cholesterol or saturated fats.

Avocados

Avocados are a fruit full of surprises. They contain 4 grams of protein, natural oils, and monounsaturated fats (the good kind). They have been cultivated for more than seven thousand years. If they are not ripe when you buy them, they will ripen in a few days in a brown paper bag kept out of the sun. You know an avocado is ripe if it feels just a little soft, like a tennis ball, when you gently squeeze it. Once ripe, the fruit's flavor is best described as "buttery."

Bamboo shoots

Bamboo shoots are the young, edible shoots of the bamboo plant. They are harvested as soon as they make their appearance above ground. The shoots are available canned. Once you open the can, rinse the shoots thoroughly to remove any bitter flavor. Bamboo shoots are sometimes available fresh at Asian specialty stores.

Basil

Look for fresh basil that is bright green and has no dark spots. Use only the leaves of the herb and not the stem, unless you are lucky enough to find small, tender Thai basil, which has flavorful stems. There are many varieties of basil to choose from, even red basil, called opal basil. Basil leaves often hold dirt. Wash them well, then wrap them in paper towels to dry. The best way to prepare basil is not to cut it with a knife. Instead, tear it with your fingers so it does not bruise.

Beans, black, cannellini, great Northern and kidney

Beans have been unearthed in Mexico dating back to 4000 BC. Beans are packed with protein, fiber, antioxidants, B vitamins, and minerals. The cannellini is an Italian white bean that is available dried or canned. The beans hold their shape even after long cooking, and the mild flavor makes them an excellent choice in soups, salads, and pasta dishes. Black, cannellini, and kidney beans are low in fat and high in appetite-satisfying flavor. Beans are commonly available dried or canned. When using dried beans, it is important to check for and remove any tiny stones or shriveled, very dark beans before preparing them. Canned beans should be put into a strainer and rinsed with cold water before being used.

Blue cheese

The distinct flavor of blue cheese is created by introducing mold into the aging process as the cheese cures. The most common varieties of blue cheese are Roquefort, Gorgonzola, Stilton, and Valdeon from Spain. Store blue cheese well-wrapped and refrigerated, and it will keep for up to 3 weeks. If you are using plastic wrap to keep the cheese fresh, you should change the wrapping every few days.

Cardamom seeds

Cardamom seeds come from the dried fruit of a member of the ginger family. Cardamom is the third most expensive spice in the world, after saffron and vanilla. There are two types that are available. Black cardamom, with its dark and wrinkled pod, is used in curries, soups, and stews. Green cardamom is used in desserts because of its sweet flavor. You can buy the seeds whole or ground.

Cayenne pepper

The cayenne pepper has very high heat content, and inside, its seeds and membrane contain a great deal of its power-punch of hotness. It is believed that cayenne peppers originated in South America and are named after the Cayenne

River in French Guiana. The dried powder made from this pepper comes from varieties that grow in Louisiana, Africa, Mexico, and Japan.

Chiles

Chile peppers are actually fruits that come from a group of plants called capsicum, and there are over one hundred varieties. Chiles are packed with vitamins A and C, can be hot or mild, and are available fresh, dried, or canned. Fresh picked chiles can be packed whole in clean glass jars and frozen without losing any of their fire. Wear rubber or disposable kitchen gloves as a precaution to keep your skin from contacting the hot oils in the chiles, which can stay on your skin for several hours. Remember, to avoid the capsaicin oil, never touch your eyes, nose, or any other part of your face or skin when working with chiles.

Jalapeños

The jalapeño is probably the most familiar of all chiles. This famous, rich, green or red hot pepper is an essential salsa ingredient. The jalapeño, which generally measures about 2½ inches long and ¾ inches wide, originated in Mexico. Available fresh or canned, it ranges from hot to very hot. You should handle it only with protective latex or kitchen gloves.

Serrano chile

Serrano is similar to jalapeño, except it is smaller and has a pointed tip. As the chile matures on the plant, its skin changes from green to bright red and then to yellow. It is packed with heat and flavor. Handle it only with protective latex or kitchen gloves. Remove the seeds and veins from the inside if you want to reduce its heat, or leave the seeds and veins if you want the chile at full heat.

Cilantro

Cilantro is an herb also known as fresh coriander or Chinese parsley. It adds a very distinct flavor to the dishes in which it is used, and as a result, some people find the flavor quite bold and the aroma too strong. It looks almost identical to flat-leaf parsley, and the two get easily confused. Wash cilantro to remove any dirt still clinging to the stems or leaves. Wrapped in paper towels, and then in plastic, it will keep for about a week in the refrigerator.

Cocoa powder

Cocoa powder is developed from beans that grow on cocoa trees in a wide variety of places like Hawaii, Brazil, Southeast Asia, South America, Africa, and Central America. Once the beans are separated from the pods, they are fermented, dried, roasted, crushed, and then ground into a paste called chocolate liquor. The liquor is hardened and ground into unsweetened cocoa powder. The powder can be blended with milk powder and sugar to create an instant cocoa mix that is not suitable for use in recipes calling for cocoa powder. Rather, you should cook with unsweetened cocoa powder for its distinct cocoa flavor. Cocoa powder will keep up to 2 years if stored in an airtight container and kept in a dark cool place.

Coconut milk

Coconut milk is made from equal parts water and shredded coconut meat. The mixture is strained through cheesecloth and then pressed to extract as much of the liquid as possible from the shredded coconut meat. The first extraction produces the richest liquid. Many cooks mistakenly assume that the liquid inside a fresh coconut is the milk. That liquid is actually coconut water. Coconut milk is sometimes available in supermarkets in convenient half-gallon refrigerated containers.

Cooking oils

Look for cold-pressed, extra-virgin, or expeller-pressed oils, which will have better flavor with fewer additives and are considered heart-healthy. All cooking oils are perishable and should be stored out of direct sunlight, kept cool, or even refrigerated. Otherwise, the oil may turn rancid. If refrigerated, return the oil to room temperature for easy pouring.

Cornmeal, stone-ground

Dried corn kernels ground on stone wheels retain some of the hull and the germ of the corn and are more nutritious than corn ground with steel blades. Stone-ground corn is available in white, yellow, and blue colors and adds a distinctive crunch to the recipes in which it is used.

Corn tortillas

Mexican tortillas usually contain just corn flour (called *masa*) and water. Look for tortillas that are made without chemical preservatives or added fats. If you have a Mexican specialty store or well-stocked supermarket near you, chances are you will find excellent tortillas. Tortillas also freeze well. Thaw them before you attempt to separate them or they are likely to split.

Curry paste

Curry paste is generally made from a variety of chiles, garlic, shallots, ginger, lemongrass, cilantro, bean or shrimp paste, coriander, cumin, salt, and pepper, among other ingredients. It is a staple in Thai and Indian cooking. Curry paste imparts a complex level of flavors to your recipes and a lot of heat. As a result it can easily overpower your dish, so use it with caution.

Curry powder

This popular blend of spices and herbs is really a product of the United Kingdom and not India. At the request of returning British subjects, Indian cooks blended spices together so that the British could have a taste of Indian cooking. Curry powder is usually, but not exclusively, a combination of cumin, cardamom, coriander seeds, mustard, cayenne pepper, and sometimes fenugreek. Turmeric is usually added for color.

Fennel

This fragrant, celery-like, pale-green vegetable makes a flavorful addition to salads and sautés. Select clean, crisp bulbs with no sign of browning. The attached feathery tops should be bright green, which indicates freshness. If stored tightly wrapped in the coldest part of your refrigerator, fennel will keep up to 1 week.

Feta cheese

Feta is one of the world's oldest cheeses. In 2005 Greece was granted the exclusive use of the name, feta. Several countries still market it, however, under the same name. Check to see if the feta you want to purchase is from Greece, hence authentic. Made from sheep's or goat's milk, and even cow's milk, this rich, tangy, low-fat cheese is pressed into squares and stored in salt-water brine. It is best used within a week of purchase.

Ginger root, fresh, ground, pickled, or crystallized

Grown for its knobby root, fresh ginger thrives in Jamaica, India, Africa, and China. It can range in color from pale green to ivory. Ginger's flavor is spicy with a hint of sweetness. Store it well-wrapped in the refrigerator or freezer. Pickled ginger is thinly sliced and preserved in a sweet vinegar solution and is a popular accompaniment to sushi. Crystallized or candied ginger is cooked in sugar syrup and coated with sugar crystals. Store in a glass jar with a lid, out of the bright light, and it will keep for several months.

Goat cheese

This popular white, tart cheese is made entirely from goat's milk. The texture ranges from creamy to crumbly. It can be found shaped in rounds, pyramids, and logs. Store it well-wrapped in the refrigerator, and it will keep for up to 10 to 14 days.

Honey

This fragrant, naturally sweet, golden nectar of the honey bee has been around for thousands of years. In fact, fossil evidence proves honeybees predate humans. When shopping for honey, look for local honey from your area. Honey can be naturally flavored with lavender, thyme, wildflower, clover, and orange blossom, depending on where it was collected. You can sometimes find honey still in the honeycomb. Remember to tightly seal the jar and to wipe the outside of it with a damp cloth to remove any drips before you store it. It is not necessary to refrigerate honey.

Lentils

The lentil, or dal as it is called in India, comes in red, brown, green, black, yellow, gray, and pink varieties—just to name a few. Lentils are packed with protein, and many vegetarians rely on lentils as an essential part of a balanced diet. It is important that you check dried lentils carefully and remove any stones or debris before cooking. Dried lentils will keep in an airtight container for a long time.

Liquid smoke

Liquid smoke actually is made from smoke. Vapors from burning wet wood chips, usually hickory, are condensed into a liquid and used to impart a smoky flavor to recipes. Look for liquid smoke made without chemical additives. A little of the liquid goes a long way in a recipe, so use it sparingly.

Mint

Mint is a variety of plant with more than thirty species—peppermint and spearmint being the most popular. Peppermint has the strongest flavor of the two. Its bright green leaves are aromatic and used for flavoring everything from salads and curries to desserts. Spearmint is milder in flavor and the leaves are a softer shade of green. Mint is easy to grow, hearty, and dries easily as a tea. Mint can easily take over your garden, however, so it is wise to keep it under control to avoid a mint invasion. Place a bunch of mint in a glass of water, place a plastic bag over the whole bunch, and store in the refrigerator for up to 1 week.

Molasses

This dark, fragrant, sweet liquid comes from raw sugar after the sugar cane is crushed and the juice is extracted and boiled. The reduction process produces raw sugar and molasses. Dark, unsulfured, or blackstrap molasses is recommended for the recipes in this book.

Mushrooms

There are thousands of varieties of this famous fungus. The range of sizes and shapes varies greatly. Mushrooms are one of the kitchen's most versatile ingredients. Cremini mushrooms, sometimes called baby portobellos, have more flavor than white mushrooms. When mature they are called portobello. Read more about mushrooms on page 80.

Nori seaweed

Nori is paper-thin sheets of dried seaweed from a plant that belongs to the algae family and dates back millions of years. Nori sheets are used as wrappers for sushi, or they can be cut into strips and used in salads and to flavor soups and stocks. The sheets can range in color from dark green and black to purple. Nori can be purchased toasted, plain, or lightly brushed with soy sauce. Purchase nori in Japanese markets, well-stocked supermarkets, or specialty shops. Nori is rich in protein, vitamins, iron, and minerals, especially calcium.

Nuts

Nuts are an edible kernel enclosed in a hard shell. Nuts are high in calcium, contain significant amounts of potassium, vitamin E, fiber, folic acid, and potassium. Brazil nuts and peanuts are actually seeds, but cashews, almonds, macadamias, pecans, pistachios, pine nuts, and walnuts are true nuts. Nuts keep their flavor and texture longer when bought in their shells. When shopping for unshelled nuts, look for ones that are chubby, uniform in color, and with the shells intact. The nuts should not rattle when you shake them. Shelled nuts come loose, canned, vacuum-packed, flavored, sugar-coated, and smoked. Nuts should be stored in the refrigerator for up to 3 months, or frozen for up to 6 months, to preserve freshness. Because nut allergies are quite serious for some people, it is advisable to inform your guests when you have prepared a recipe with nuts.

Oregano

Oregano is a member of the mint family and a cousin to thyme and marjoram. Its name means "joy of the mountain." Dried or fresh, this pungent herb is full of flavor. It is perfect for pizza, tomato sauces, tofu dishes, chile, and vegetables. Dried Mediterranean oregano is sometimes available on the stem, or in jars. When shopping for fresh oregano, look for bright green leaves that are not wilted. Refrigerated and wrapped in wax paper or plastic, it will stay fresh for up to 1 week.

Panko bread crumbs

These Japanese bread crumbs are made from crust-less bread that is dried and ground to create large coarse and crispy crumbs. Panko absorbs liquid and spices very well and still keeps its crunch. Look for panko crumbs that contain no partially hydrogenated oils or preservatives.

Paprika, smoked

This spice is a blend of fresh red peppers that are smoked over wood fires, then dried and ground. The paprika develops a rich taste with a hint of smoke and an appealing deep color.

Parmigiano-Reggiano

Sometimes referred to as the "King of Cheeses," Parmigiano-Reggiano is one of Italy's most famous cheeses. It has been made for more than five hundred years, but the official recipe used today in Parma and Reggio Emilia was only established in 1955. It is lower in fat and cholesterol than many other cheeses. You can recognize it because its name is stamped into the rind of the cheese. Buy it in a wedge and grate it as needed to maintain peak flavor. To store, wrap it in wax paper and then a layer of aluminum foil and keep it in the coldest part of the refrigerator. Parmigiano-Reggiano is expensive. Consider your budget when shopping for it. You may substitute other Parmesan cheeses, but avoid buying them already grated.

Plum tomatoes

Plum tomatoes, also called Roma tomatoes or pear tomatoes because of their shape, are available in supermarkets year round. Plum tomatoes do not contain of lot of seeds, which makes them desirable for sauces. When shopping for plum tomatoes, look for a rich, red color and stay away from tomatoes with dark spots or bruises. A tomato will lose most of its flavor if stored in the refrigerator.

Polenta, instant

Polenta is cornmeal ground into medium or coarse grind. Stone-ground polenta is also available, but it can quickly turn rancid, so it is recommended that you tightly seal it and keep it refrigerated until ready to use. Polenta is a good source of fiber and B vitamins and can be served soft or firm and with a generous grating of cheese and butter or olive oil. It is also good with chopped sun-dried tomatoes, pitted olives, or sautéed onions.

Quinoa

Quinoa (pronounced Keen-Waa) dates back roughly 5000 years to the Aztec and Inca farmers. The quinoa plant is rugged and can grow at very high altitudes. The stalks can reach up to 6½ feet high. Technically not a grain, quinoa is a cousin to beets, spinach, and Swiss chard. It is prepared exactly like rice and has a mild, nutty flavor. It is a near perfect combination of fiber, balanced amino-acids, B-vitamins, minerals, iron, and protein. Make sure to buy rinsed quinoa, which has been soaked to remove the bitter outer coating so that it's ready to cook. Always give quinoa an additional thorough rinsing with a hand strainer just before cooking.

Red pepper flakes, crushed

Dried, hot red peppers are crushed into flakes. Red pepper flakes have plenty of heat so use them with caution.

Salt

Salt is produced by evaporating sea water. It is also mined from salt mines. It is probably the oldest and most common seasoning in cooking. Add enough, and a dish will be memorable; add too much, and a dish will be ruined. For the recipes in this book, choose from the many varieties of unrefined, minimally processed salts, such as *fleur de sel* and other sea salts which can be fine or coarse-grain. Table salt is a more processed variety and may have iodine added (iodized). Another popular salt is kosher salt, which has a coarse grain. It is available in most supermarkets. You are free to use whichever salt you would like for the recipes in this book.

Savoy cabbage

Savoy cabbage has a mellow flavor and a loose, full head of crinkled leaves. Its color can range from dark to pale green. It will keep up to 10 days if well wrapped and refrigerated.

Sesame seeds

These tiny, nutty, very flavorful seeds are believed to be the first recorded seasoning, dating back to 300 B.C. Sesame seeds were introduced to the American kitchen by African slaves. Sesame seeds may be brown, white, black, or yellow. Toasting the seeds brings out extra flavor. Their nutty, slightly sweet flavor works as well in savory dishes as it does in desserts. The seeds can be pressed into a paste similar to peanut butter. Sesame oil is high in polyunsaturated fats, and the high smoke point (420°F) makes it a great oil for frying.

Shortening, vegetable

A solid fat made from, among other ingredients, corn, soybean, palm, or coconut oils. Shop for vegetable shortening that has not been chemically transformed into a solid through hydrogenation. This type of shortening is harder to find but is worth the effort to avoid unhealthy, hydrogenated shortening. Read shortening labels carefully.

Spelt flour

Spelt flour is higher in protein, sweeter, and has a more pronounced nutty flavor than whole-wheat flour. Spelt contains a broad collection of nutrients and has gained new-found popularity in recent years, not only for its taste, but also for its supposed health benefits. Spelt dates back thousands of years and has been grown in the United States for only the last 100 years. It looks like wheat, but actually it is quite different. The outside husk is tougher, which protects its nutritional content. Some people with wheat allergies find it a winning substitute. Spelt does contain some gluten so it is not recommended for gluten-free recipes.

Sugar, raw (turbinado)

Turbinado sugar is an alternative to white processed sugar. Raw sugar, like white sugar, is harvested from sugar cane, but it is less processed and contains a few less calories per teaspoon. The sugar crystals are coarse and blond colored. The flavor of raw sugar has a hint of molasses.

Sunflower seeds

The brilliant, golden sunflower certainly lives up to its name. At the center of the flower are the seeds that, when pressed, are prized for their oil, which is very high in polyunsaturated fat. The seeds also are very popular because they are high in protein and are filled with vitamins and minerals. The oil is perishable and should be kept in a dark, cool place once opened.

Tabasco sauce

Tabasco is the trade name for a bottled hot sauce that originated around 1870 and is made from Tabasco peppers. The sauce is actually fermented in large casks on Avery Island in Louisiana. The sauce is extremely hot; use it with caution and think of it as liquid heat.

Tamari sauce

Tamari made from soybeans is similar to soy sauce, but it is thicker in consistency. Many people prefer the mellower flavor of tamari to soy sauce.

Tapioca

Tapioca is a starchy powder that has been extracted from the root of the yucca plant. It is used as a thickening agent in baking and is sometimes used in soups or as a dessert.

Tempeh

Tempeh is made from cooked and fermented soybeans pressed into square cakes. Its nutty flavor and wide range of uses in vegetarian cooking plus its high-protein content make it a delicious substitute for meat. Like tofu, it absorbs the flavor of the other ingredients in the dish. It crumbles nicely into sauces and chile and comes in a variety of flavors.

Tofu, firm, extra-firm, silken

Tofu is sometimes referred to as bean curd, or soybean curd. It is made from curdled soy milk in a process similar to cheese making. The curds are strained and pressed into cakes. The whey, or liquid that drains off the curds, determines how firm or soft the finished tofu will be. The result is a smooth, creamy, mild-tasting, protein-packed ingredient that takes on the flavor of the other ingredients in the recipe. Tofu is a protein alternative in many vegetarian dishes. It is available in regular, low-fat, and nonfat varieties. It can come flavored, smoked, or plain. The most common types of tofu are extra-firm, firm, and soft. Silken tofu is light and creamy and the lowest in calories. Tofu is perishable. It must be refrigerated until you are ready to use it. Choose the freshness date on the package that is the furthest from the date you purchase it. You should cover and store it in the refrigerator for no more than 1 week. If you purchase fresh tofu packed in water, replace the water every day and it will keep up to one week. Tofu is low in calories, contains lots of calcium, and has no cholesterol.

Tomatillos

Tomatillos are a small, green, tart fruit of the nightshade family, which includes tomatoes, potatoes, and red and green peppers. They are often confused with green tomatoes. The papery outer husk needs to be peeled away and removed before using, and then the fruit has to be washed to remove any sticky residue. Look for firm, solid tomatillos that fill the skin completely. They will keep in the vegetable drawer in the refrigerator for up to 2 weeks.

Turmeric, ground

India is the largest producer of turmeric in the world. It is a rhizome, or underground stem, that's picked young, cleaned, and dried in the sun, then ground into a golden powder. Turmeric is used as a fabric dye as well as a spice. Be careful! It will stain, and the stains are not easy to remove.

Vanilla extract, pure

Vanilla extract contains the flavor and delicate aroma of vanilla beans. The vanilla bean is the rare fruit of a variety of very pale green orchids. The process of extracting the vanilla liquid is labor intensive and accounts for it expensive price. The cultivation of vanilla dates back to the Aztecs, who used it to enhance the flavor of chocolate. The extract is blended with alcohol to preserve its delicate flavor. If possible, shop for pure vanilla extract rather than imitation vanilla for the recipes in this book. Pure vanilla is generally more expensive than imitation, so you should keep your budget in mind when selecting.

Vinegar, balsamic, rice, apple cider, white, red wine, coconut

Vinegar is made from the fermented liquid of fruits and other plants that contain natural sugars. Vinegar has been used for thousands of years, not only for cooking but also as an all-natural cleaning product; it has even been used as a hair conditioner. Balsamic vinegar is sweet, tangy, and very versatile in the kitchen. Balsamic traditionally comes from the Emilia-Romagna region of northern Italy and has been produced for over a thousand years.

Wasabi

Wasabi is a perennial herb from the same family as horseradish, mustard, and cabbage plants. The spicy wasabi plant grows wild in or around the banks of mountain streams in Japan and is very costly to cultivate. As a result, fresh wasabi is rarely obtained outside of Japan. Wasabi paste is a blend of horseradish, mustard, and green coloring. Wasabi powder is available in Asian specialty markets and can be blended with water into a paste. Wasabi is one of the most popular condiments for sushi.

Wheat germ

The wheat germ is the part of the wheat kernel that grows into a plant. It is high in protein, contains vitamin E, omega-3, folic acid, and is also an excellent source of fiber. Wheat germ is perishable and, after it is opened, should be stored in the refrigerator to preserve its freshness. Wheat germ is used in breads, as a breakfast cereal, in blended drinks, and it is very popular because of its high concentration of essential nutrients and anti-oxidants. Toasted wheat germ is recommended for the recipes in this book.

Whole-wheat flour

Whole-wheat flour contains the whole kernel of wheat ground into flour. As a result it retains more nutrients than bleached white flour. It can give breads and pastries increased density and a nuttier taste than lighter flours.

Yogurt, whole milk, soy

Yogurt can also be made from the milk of cows, goats, or even buffalo, or soy beans and even coconut milk. Purchase yogurt as far ahead as possible from the expiration date on the container and keep it refrigerated.

You can use the chart below to convert from U.S. measurements to the metric system.

Weight

1 ounce = 28 grams

½ pound (8 ounces) = 227 grams

1 pound = .45 kilogram

2.2 pounds = 1 kilogram

Liquid volume

1 teaspoon = 5 milliliters

1 tablespoon = 15 milliliters

1 fluid ounce = 30 milliliters

1 cup = 240 milliliters (.24 liter)

1 pint = 480 milliliters (.48 liter)

1 quart = 950 milliliters (.95 liter)

Length

¼ inch = .6 centimeter

½ inch = 1.25 centimeters

1 inch = 2.5 centimeters

Temperature

100°F = 40°C

110°F = 45°C

212°F = 100°C (boiling point of water)

350°F = 180°C

375°F = 190°C

400°F = 200°C

425°F = 220°C

450°F = 235°C

(To convert temperatures in Fahrenheit to Celsius, subtract 32 and multiply by .56)

METRIC CONVERSION CHART

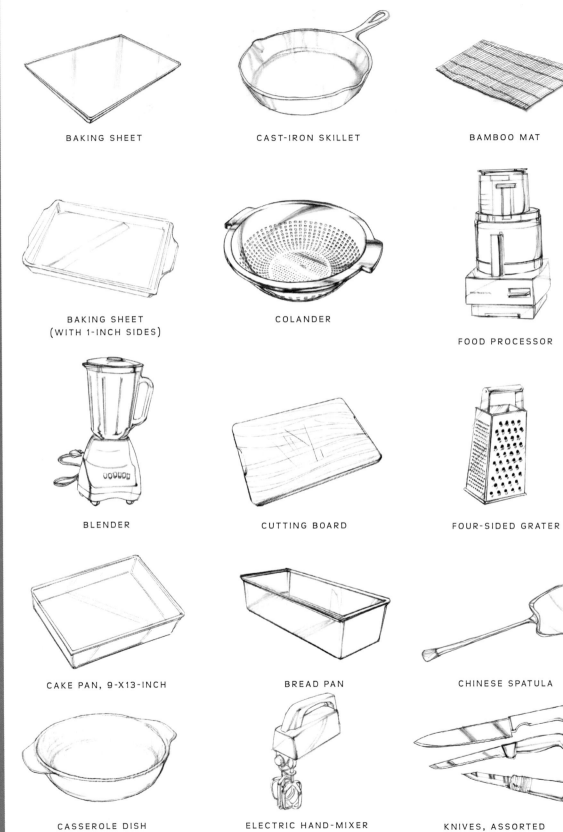

BAKING SHEET

CAST-IRON SKILLET

BAMBOO MAT

BAKING SHEET
(WITH 1-INCH SIDES)

COLANDER

FOOD PROCESSOR

BLENDER

CUTTING BOARD

FOUR-SIDED GRATER

CAKE PAN, 9-X13-INCH

BREAD PAN

CHINESE SPATULA

CASSEROLE DISH

ELECTRIC HAND-MIXER

KNIVES, ASSORTED

LATEX GLOVES

MUFFIN TIN, 12-CUP

RUBBER SPATULAS

MEASURING CUPS

PANCAKE GRIDDLE

SAUCEPANS WITH LIDS,
ASSORTED SIZES

MEASURING SPOONS

PASTRY BRUSH

LARGE METAL SLOTTED SPOON

FLOUR SIFTER

GLASS JARS

PASTRY BAG

MIXING BOWLS

ROLLING PIN

SPATULA

RICE PADDLE

TONGS

VEGETABLE BRUSH

STOCK POT

VEGETABLE/POTATO PEELER

WOODEN SPOONS

HAND STRAINER

WHISK

WOK

12-INCH ROUND PIE
PAN/BAKING DISH

WIRE COOLING RACK

INDEX

Bold numbers are for pages with photographs.

A

agave nectar, 183

agave syrup, 183

allspice, 183

almond milk, 183
  French's Toast, **10,** 12–13, **13**
  TLC Dressing, 96

almonds. *See also* nuts
  Smart Bars, **68,** 69–70, **71**
  TLC Dressing, 96

apples
  New Waldorf Salad, **88,** 90–91

asparagus
  Spring Table Pasta, **102,** 104–5

avocados, 183
  California-on-a-Roll, **54,** 55–57, **56, 57**
  Guacamole, 62–63
  Make-a-Scene Pasta, 111–12, **113**
  Make-a-Scene Pasta Raw Version, **114,** 115–16
  New Bean Soup, 74–75

B

bamboo shoots, 183
  Curried Vegetable Stir-Fry, **118,** 120–21

bananas
  Banana-Berry Blender Bender, **48,** 49
  Banana Slap, **42,** 43

basil, 184

beans, 184. *See also specific kinds*
  Bite-Me Chile, **84,** 85–86

beets, 31
  New BLT Sandwich, 30–31, **31**

bell peppers, **163**
  Ratatouille, 125–28, **126, 129**

berries. *See also specific kinds*
  Banana-Berry Blender Bender, **48,** 49
  dried

  Smart Bars, **68,** 69–70, **71**

beverages, 40–49
  Banana-Berry Blender Bender, **48,** 49
  Banana Slap, **42,** 43
  Ginger Ale, **46,** 47
  Ginger Syrup, 45
    Strawberry Lassi, 44

Bite-Me Chile, **84,** 85–86

black beans, 184
  Black Bean Hash Browns, 25–26, **27**
  New Bean Soup, **72,** 74–75

blueberries. *See also* berries
  Banana-Berry Blender Bender, **48,** 49
  Blueberry and Dried Cherry Crumble, 179–80, **181**

blue cheese, 184
  Red, White, and Blue Cheese Potato Salad, **92,** 93–94

breads
  Cheddar Cheese and Jalapeño Corn Muffins, 19–20, **21**
  Quinoa and Whole-Wheat Bread, **14, 17,** 15–17
  recipes using, 87
    French's Toast, **10,** 12–13, **13**
    New BLT Sandwich, 30–31, **31**
    New Tempeh Burger, **36,** 37–39, **38, 39**
    Sloppy Jane, **32,** 33–34

breakfast, 10–27
  Cheddar Cheese and Jalapeño Corn Muffins, 19–20, **21**
  Crispy Tortillas and Scrambled Eggs Mex-Tex, **22,** 23–24
  French's Toast, **10,** 12–13, **13**
  Quinoa and Whole-Wheat Bread, **14,** 15–17

C

cabbage
  buying and storing, 100
  Red Cool Slaw, 99–100, **99**

savoy, 191

California-on-a-Roll, **54,** 55–57, **56, 57**

cannellini beans, 184. *See also* beans

Minestrone, **78,** 79–80

Red, White, and Blue Cheese Potato Salad,
92, 93–94

cardamom seeds, 184

carrots

California-on-a-Roll, **54,** 55–57, **56, 57**

Carrot and Mint Chutney, **160,** 161–62

Crispy Cucumber and Carrot Pickles, **148,**
149–50

Curried Vegetable Stir-Fry, **118,** 120–21

Homemade Vegetable Stock, **76,** 77

Sloppy Jane, **32,** 33–34

Spring Table Pasta, **102,** 104–5

cashews. *See also* nuts

Sweet-and-Sour Tofu Stir-Fry, **122,** 123–24

cayenne pepper, 184–85

celery, about, 94

chanterelle mushrooms, 80, **83.** *See also*
mushrooms

cheddar cheese. *See also* cheese

Cheddar Cheese and Jalapeño Corn
Muffins, 19–20, **21**

cheese

Cheddar Cheese and Jalapeño Corn
Muffins, 19–20, **21**

Red, White, and Blue Cheese Potato Salad,
92, 93–94

Spinach Pie, **140,** 141–44

Three-Cheese Polenta Pie, **106,** 107–8, **109**

cherries, dried

Blueberry and Dried Cherry Crumble,
179–80, **181**

chiles, 185. *See also* jalapeño chiles, serrano
chile

Bite-Me Chile, **84,** 85–86

chocolate

Chocolate Cream Frosting, 170

Chocolate Cupcakes, **166,** 167–68, **169**

Chunky Mushroom Gravy, 134–35

Chutney, Carrot and Mint, **160,** 161–62

cilantro, 185

cocoa powder, 186

coconut milk, 186

French's Toast, **10,** 12–13, **13**

condiments, 146–63

Cookies, Snappy Ginger, **176,** 177–78

cooking oils, 186

corn

Curried Vegetable Stir-Fry, **118,** 120–21

cornmeal, 186. *See also* polenta

Cheddar Cheese and Jalapeño Corn Muffins,
19–20, **21**

Crispy Cucumber and Carrot Pickles, **148,**
149–50

Crispy Tortillas and Scrambled Eggs Mex-Tex,
22, 23–24

Croutons, Seasoned, 87

cucumbers

California-on-a-Roll, **54,** 55–57, **56**

Crispy Cucumber and Carrot Pickles, **148,**
149–50

Cucumber and Radish Relish, 151–52, **153**

cupcakes, 168

Chocolate Cupcakes, **166,** 167–68, **169**

Vanilla Cupcakes, **172,** 173–74, **175**

Curry, 121

Curried Vegetable Stir-Fry, **118,** 120–21

paste, 187

powder, 187

D

dates

Banana-Berry Blender Bender, **48,** 49

Banana Slap, **42,** 43

New Waldorf Salad, **88,** 90–91

Smart Bars, **68,** 69–70, **71**

desserts, 164–81

  Blueberry and Dried Cherry Crumble, 179–80, **181**

  Chocolate Cupcakes, 167–68, **169**

  Snappy Ginger Cookies, **176,** 177–78

  Vanilla Cupcakes, 173–74, **175**

drinks. *See* beverages

E

Eat Loaf, **130,** 131–33, **133**

eggplant

  Ratatouille, 125–28, **126, 129**

eggs

  Crispy Tortillas and Scrambled Eggs Mex-Tex, **22,** 23–24

equipment, kitchen, 198–200

F

fennel, **91,** 187

  New Waldorf Salad, **88,** 90–91

feta cheese, 187

  Spinach Pie, **140,** 141–44

French's Toast, **10,** 12–13, **13**

frosting

  Chocolate Cream Frosting, 170

  Vanilla Frosting, 171

fruit, dried. *See also specific kinds*

  New Waldorf Salad, **88,** 90–91

  Smart Bars, **68,** 69–70, **71**

G

ginger, **139,** 187

  Ginger Ale, **46,** 47

  Ginger Syrup, 45

  Snappy Ginger Cookies, **176,** 177–78

goat cheese, 188

  New Waldorf Salad, **88,** 90–91

Gravy, Chunky Mushroom, 134–35

great Northern beans, 184. *See also* beans

green beans

  Curried Vegetable Stir-Fry, **118,** 120–21

Guacamole, 62–63

H

Hodgepodge, **136,** 137–38

Homemade Vegetable Stock, **76,** 77

honey, 188

I

ingredients, 183–95

Instant Polenta, 110

J

jalapeño chiles, **158,** 185. *See also* chiles

  Cheddar Cheese and Jalapeño Corn Muffins, 19–20, **21**

  Salsa Verde, 157–58, **159**

K

kale, 100, 101

  Red Cool Slaw, **98,** 99–100

ketchup, 34

  Ketchup, **154,** 155–56

kidney beans, 184. *See also* beans

kitchen equipment and utensils, 198–200

kitchen essentials, 182–200

knife safety, 9

L

leeks

  Spinach Pie, **140,** 141–44

lentils, 188

  Hodgepodge, **136,** 137–38

lettuce

  New BLT Sandwich, 30–31, **31**

liquid smoke, 188

M

main dishes, 118–45

Make-a-Scene Pasta, 111–12, **113**

Make-a-Scene Pasta Raw Version, **114,** 115–16

metric conversions, 197

Minestrone, **78,** 79–80

mint, 188

molasses, 189

Muffins, Corn, Cheddar Cheese and
    Jalapeño, 19–20, **21**

mushrooms, 80, 189. *See also specific kinds*
  Chunky Mushroom Gravy, 134–35
  Eat Loaf, **130,** 131–34, **133**
  Homemade Vegetable Stock, **76,** 77
  Minestrone, **78,** 79–80
  Sloppy Jane, **32,** 33–34
  Sweet-and-Sour Tofu Stir-Fry, **122,** 123–24
  Three-Cheese Polenta Pie, **106,** 107–8, **109**

N

New Bean Soup, 74–75

New BLT Sandwich, 30–31, **31**

New Tempeh Burger, **36,** 37–39, **38, 39**

New Waldorf Salad, **88,** 90–91

nori seaweed, 189

nuts, 189. *See also specific kinds*
  Blueberry and Dried Cherry Crumble, 179–
    80, **181**
  New Waldorf Salad, **88,** 90–91

O

oats
  Blueberry and Dried Cherry Crumble, 179–
    80, **181**
  Smart Bars, **68,** 69–70, **71**

onion, **35, 143**

oregano, 190

oyster mushrooms, 80, **81**

P

panko bread crumbs, 190

paprika, smoked, 190

Parmesan cheese, 190

Parmigiano-Reggiano, 190

party foods, 60–71

pasta
  Make-a-Scene Pasta, 111–12, **113**
  Make-a-Scene Pasta
    Raw version, **114,** 115–16
  Minestrone, **78,** 79–80
    Spring Table Pasta, **102,** 104–5

pastry bag replacement, 170

peanut butter
  Banana Slap, **42,** 43
  Smart Bars, **68,** 69–70, **71**

peppers, **163**

phyllo dough, 145
  Spinach Pie, **140,** 141–44

pickles
  Crispy Cucumber and Carrot Pickles, **148,**
    149–50
  Cucumber and Radish Relish, 151–52, **153**

pies
  Spinach Pie, **140,** 141–44
  Three-Cheese Polenta Pie, **106,** 107–8, **109**

plum tomatoes, 190. *See also* tomatoes

polenta, 191
  Instant Polenta, 110
  Three-Cheese Polenta Pie, **106,** 107–8, **109**

potatoes, 94, **95**
  Black Bean Hash Browns, 25–26, **27**
  Red, White, and Blue Cheese Potato Salad,
    92, 93–94

Q

quinoa, 191
  Hodgepodge, **136,** 137–38
  Quinoa, 18, **18**
    Quinoa and Whole-Wheat Bread, **14, 17,** 15–17

R

Radish Relish, Cucumber and Radish Relish,
  151–52, **153**

Rancho Dressing, 97

Ratatouille, 125–28, **126, 129**

Red Cool Slaw, **98,** 99–100

red pepper flakes, crushed, 191

Red, White, and Blue Cheese Potato Salad, **92,** 93–94

relishes

  Cucumber and Radish Relish, 151–52, **153**

  Ketchup, **154,** 155–56

  Salsa Verde, 157–58, **159**

rice

  California-on-a-Roll, **54,** 55–57, **56, 57**

  Sushi Rice, 52–53

S

safety, 9

salad dressings

  Rancho Dressing, 97

  TLC Dressing, 96

salads, 88–101

  New Waldorf Salad, **88,** 90–91

    Red Cool Slaw, **98,** 99–100

    Red, White, and Blue Cheese Potato Salad, **92,** 93–94

Salsa Verde, 157–58, **159**

salt, 191

sandwiches, 28–39

  New BLT Sandwich, 30–31, 31

  New Tempeh Burger, **36,** 37–39, **38, 39**

  Sloppy Jane, **32,** 33–34

sauces. *See also* relishes

  Chunky Mushroom Gravy, 134–35

  Ketchup, **154,** 155–56

  Salsa Verde, 157–58, **159**

savoy cabbage, 191

scallions, **143**

Seasoned Croutons, 87

serrano chiles, 185. *See also* chiles

sesame seeds, 192

shiitake mushrooms, 80, **82**

  Sweet-and-Sour Tofu Stir-Fry, **122,** 123–24

shopping tips

  cabbage, 100

  kale, 100

    ketchup, 34

    mushrooms, 80

  potatoes, 94

shortening, vegetable, 192

side dishes, 146–63

Sloppy Jane, **32,** 33–34

Smart Bars, **68,** 69–70, **71**

Snappy Ginger Cookies, **176,** 177–78

soups, 72–87

  Homemade Vegetable Stock, **76,** 77

  Minestrone, **78,** 79–80

  New Bean Soup, 74–75

spelt flour, 192

spinach

  Spinach Pie, **140,** 141–44

Spring Table Pasta, **102,** 104–5

storage tips

  cabbage, 100

  kale, 100

  potatoes, 94

strawberries. *See also* berries

  Banana-Berry Blender Bender, **48,** 49

  Strawberry Lassi, 44

sugar, raw, 192

sunflower seeds, 192

sushi, 50–59

  California-on-a-Roll, **54,** 55–57, **56, 57**

  Sushi Rice, 52–53

  tips for making, 57

Sweet-and-Sour Tofu Stir-Fry, **122,** 123–24

Swiss chard

  Spring Table Pasta, **102,** 104–5

T

Tabasco sauce, 193

tamari sauce, 193

tapioca, 193

tempeh, 193

  Bite-Me Chile, **84,** 85–86

  California-on-a-Roll, **54,** 55–57, **56, 57**

  New Tempeh Burger, **36,** 37–39, **38, 39**

  Tempeh Fingers, **58,** 59

  Tempeh Nuggets, **64,** 65–66

Three-Cheese Polenta Pie, **106,** 107–8, **109**

tips

  beans, canned, 75

  beets, handling, 31

  cupcakes, 168

  curry paste, 121

  ketchup buying, 34

  mushrooms, 80

  pastry bag replacement, 170

  phyllo dough, 145

  potatoes, buying and storing, 94

  sushi making, 57

    vegetable stock storing, 77

TLC Dressing, 96

tofu, 193

  Eat Loaf, **130,** 131–34, **133**

  Sweet-and-Sour Tofu Stir-Fry, **122,** 123–24

  TLC Dressing, 96

tomatillos, **67,** 194

  Salsa Verde, 157–58, **159**

tomatoes, 117

  Bite-Me Chile, **84,** 85–86

  Eat Loaf, **130,** 131–34, **133**

  Ketchup, **154,** 155–56

  Make-a-Scene Pasta, 111–12, **113**

  Make-a-Scene Pasta Raw Version, **114,** 115–16

  New BLT Sandwich, 30–31, **31**

  plum, 190

  Ratatouille, 125–28, **126, 129**

  Red Cool Slaw, **98,** 99–100

  Spring Table Pasta, **102,** 104–5

tortillas, 186

  chips

    Guacamole, 62–63

    Crispy Tortillas and Scrambled Eggs

      Mex-Tex, **22,** 23–24

turbinado sugar, 192

turmeric, ground, 194

U

utensils, kitchen, 198–200

V

vanilla extract, 194

    Vanilla Cupcakes, **172,** 173–74, **175**

    Vanilla Frosting, 171

vegetables. *See also specific kinds*

  Curried Vegetable Stir-Fry, **118,** 120–21

  Homemade Vegetable Stock, **76,** 77

  Minestrone, **78,** 79–80

vinegar, 194

W

wasabi, 195

wheat germ, 195

whole-wheat flour, 195

Y

yogurt, 195

  Banana Slap, **42,** 43

  Red, White, and Blue Cheese Potato

    Salad, **92,** 93–94

  Strawberry Lassi, 44

Z

zucchini

  Make-a-Scene Pasta Raw Version, **114,** 115–16

  Ratatouille, 125–28, **126, 129**

  Spring Table Pasta, **102,** 104–5